THE CHOICE

A Fable of Free Trade and Protectionism

THE CHOICE

A Fable of Free Trade and Protectionism

RUSSELL D. ROBERTS
Washington University in St. Louis

PRENTICE HALL, Englewood Cliffs, NJ 07632

Library of Congress Cataloging–in–Publication Data

Roberts, Russell D.
    The choice :   a fable of free trade and protectionism/Russell D. Roberts.
        p.   cm.
    1. Free trade.   2. Protectionism.   3. Free trade--United States.
    4. Protectionism—United States.   5. Ricardo, David,   1772-1823.
    I. Title.
    HF1713.R615   1994

                                                      93-44899
                                                      CIP

Acquisition Editor   Stephen Dietrich
Production Editor   Maureen Wilson
Cover Designer   Bruce Kenselaar
Manufacturing Buyer   Patrice Fraccio
Editorial Assistant   Liz Becker

Photo on p. viii courtesy of Bettman.

Photo on p. ix courtesy of Culver Pictures.

 © Published by Prentice-Hall, Inc.
A Paramount Communications Company
Englewood Cliffs, NJ 07632

Printed in the United States of America
10   9   8

ISBN   0-13-083008-9

Prentice-Hall International (UK) Limited, *London*
Prentice-Hall of Australia Pty. Limited, *Sydney*
Prentice-Hall Canada Inc., *Toronto*
Prentice-Hall Hispanoamericana, S.A., *Mexico*
Prentice-Hall of India Private Limited, *New Delhi*
Prentice-Hall of Japan, Inc., *Tokyo*
Simon & Schuster Asia Pte Ltd., *Singapore*
Editora Prentice Hall do Brasil, Ltda., *Rio de Janeiro*

To my parents, Ted and Shirley Roberts,
who taught me to love words, life, and the world

CONTENTS

DAVID RICARDO

David Ricardo was an English economist, widely regarded as one of the greatest practitioners of the deductive method of analysis in economics. He was born in London on April 18, 1772, to orthodox Jewish parents. Ricardo became estranged from his family when he became a Unitarian and married a Quaker in 1793. He was first employed by his father in the London Stock Exchange in 1786 and operated there independently from 1793 to 1816. By 1813, he had amassed a large fortune and retired from business. He served in the House of Commons as the member from Porttarlington from 1819 until his death in Gloucestershire on September 11, 1823. Ricardo's most famous work, *On the Principles of Political Economy and Taxation*, first appeared in 1817.   *Encyclopedia Americana*

ED JOHNSON

Ed Johnson was born in 1917 in Star, Illinois. He received a degree in engineering from the University of Illinois in 1939. Johnson served in the U.S. Army during World War II achieving the rank of Major. He earned a Silver Star for gallantry in action at Omaha Beach in the D-Day operation. After the war, he returned to Star Illinois to work in the Stellar Television Company. He was named President of the company in 1955. He married Martha Hellman in 1948. The Johnsons had two children, Steven born in 1949, and Susan born in 1954.

AUTHOR'S NOTE

The Stellar Television Company, the towns of Star, Clarksville, and Clearview Illinois, the citizens of those towns described here, and Congressman Frank Bates, are products of the author's imagination. Any resemblance of these characters to any persons living or dead, is purely coincidental. All of the other companies and people are real. I have tried to portray them and the American economy as accurately as possible. Sources are found at the conclusion of the story, in Chapter Fifteen.

CHAPTER ONE

Minutes of the Heavenly Court: Soul of David Ricardo

INITIAL TRIAL
DATE: September 11, 1823

MAGISTRATE: Please state pertinent biographical detail.

DEFENDANT: I was born in 1772 and given the name David Ricardo. My mother, peace be upon her, named me after King David, writer of psalms, sweet singer of Israel. She—

MAGISTRATE: Mr. Ricardo. Less lyricism. More facts. Occupation?

DEFENDANT: I was chiefly a financier, then later, a politician.

MAGISTRATE: Speak up, Mr. Ricardo. Your occupation will not be held against you. What do you consider your most important achievement while you were alive?

DEFENDANT: My theory of comparative advantage. Outlined in my 1817 book, *Principles of Political Economy and Taxation,* the theory showed how nations benefit from free trade. In addition, as a Member of the British Parliament, I spoke numerous times on the dangers of protectionism and the benefits of free trade.

MAGISTRATE: Were your views heeded?

1

DEFENDANT: Not yet, but in time I believe—

MAGISTRATE: That will be all, Mr. Ricardo. You are sentenced to a period of wandering until further evidence is brought to the attention of this court.

REQUEST FOR RE-TRIAL
DATE: December 18, 1846

MAGISTRATE: Mr. Ricardo. You have requested this hearing to put forward additional evidence you believe relevant to your case.

DEFENDANT: Yes. I am happy to report that down below, my native country of England has abolished the Corn Laws which protected British farmers from foreign competition. I request that the court consider reopening my case.

MAGISTRATE: Request dismissed. It is too early to tell if this change is temporary or permanent. In addition, do not virtually all nations outside of Britain still practise extensive trade restrictions?

DEFENDANT: Yes, but—

MAGISTRATE: That will be all, Mr. Ricardo.

REQUEST FOR TOUCHING DOWN
DATE: July 13, 1960

MAGISTRATE: Mr. Ricardo. You have requested an opportunity to intervene in human affairs to remove your status as a wanderer. What evidence justifies your request?

DEFENDANT: I believe the United States is about to embark on a policy of protectionism that will destroy the American economy. I request one evening on earth to help put America on the path of freer trade and prosperity.

MAGISTRATE: Request granted. You realize, Mr. Ricardo, that a wanderer is allowed only one period of touching down during the probationary period.

DEFENDANT: Yes, sir. I feel confident that—

MAGISTRATE: That will be all, Mr. Ricardo. Good luck. And Godspeed.

CHAPTER TWO

The Challenge of Foreign Competition

"When our factory opened, a worker made $50 per week and over at Willie's Appliance Store a Stellar television cost $250. So it took a worker five weeks of work to earn a television. Today, the average worker in that plant makes $100 per week and Willie gets $200 for a Stellar television. Two weeks of work to earn a television. That's how I measure our success—how many hours it takes one of you to earn one of our products. That number has been falling since the first year of operation."

That was Ed Johnson talking back in 1959, a year before I touched down. Ed's the Chief Executive Officer of Stellar Television Company. Their headquarters are in Star, Illinois, the destination for my one night back on earth. If you had been dead for 137 years and had one evening back on earth, you probably wouldn't head for a town of 100,000 people in Illinois. But Ed Johnson and Star hold the key to my future and America's. I thought you'd like to get to know Ed and his company before I touched down.

Ed was talking at the annual company picnic, held every year in Johnson Park. They named the park for his father, who started the company. Ed always has a great time. He brings the family, tears his pants sliding into second in the softball game, and eats a lot of fried chicken and potato salad. Ed gets along fine with the workers—he worked in the plant in high school before heading off to study engineering. Stellar has three other factories around the state, but the one in Star's the biggest. In a good month, the 5,000 workers in Star make 80,000 televisions.

As you can tell from Ed's speech, Ed was pretty proud of his company. But walking home from the picnic, his wife Martha sensed something was wrong. She waited until their two children ran up ahead and out of earshot.

"What's bothering you, dear?"

"Foreign competition. Japanese televisions are coming into America. I almost had to lay off workers this month. And I may have to lower wages and break the string I talked about this afternoon."

4

"Oh, honey, you're teasing. People know that "Made in Japan" means junk. No one is going to buy a Japanese television."

"Some are buying them now."

The next morning, after a restless night, Ed drove into Chicago and took a plane to Washington. He met with his Congressman, Frank Bates. He asked for a limit on imports of Japanese televisions. Eliminating foreign competition would keep the jobs and wages of his workers safe.

"Well now, Ed, I just don't know. You've been good to me, always helping out with the campaign and I appreciate that. But this kind of bill is tricky. People want a level playing field. Competition is the American way of life. Playing tough with the Japanese isn't going to look good."

"That's nonsense, Frank. We invented the television. The Japanese stole it from us. Now they're stealing our jobs. If good jobs go to Japan, what will we replace them with? What will happen to Star? And what will happen to the companies around Chicago that supply us? If Stellar Television closes, the trouble doesn't end in Star, it just begins there! We can't let the Japanese get ahead. They'll get all the future inventions in electronics if our television industry disappears."

"I hear what you're saying, Ed. Hey, I fought in the Pacific. Listen, Ed. There's serious talk of me making a real run at the White House. I don't need some trade bill around my neck. Let me get in the White House and then I can help."

"How are you going to run for President if people in your home district are having trouble making ends meet? A bill like this can put you in the White House. You just have to explain it right. Buying American will make America rich again."

"It sounds better when you put it that way. Let me think it over."

Frank Bates thought it over and decided to sponsor a bill banning foreign televisions. Every month another 80,000 televisions came off the line at Stellar Television, and every month there was more talk of Congressman Bates being President Bates some day. His trade bill banning imports of televisions passed. He started speaking about a plan to keep out all foreign products entirely. Pass on the benefits to other industries, not just televisions. That plan became the centerpiece of his Presidential campaign. Ed Johnson did a lot of traveling and speaking for Frank Bates, defending protectionism.

By the summer of 1960, Frank Bates was even money to get his party's nomination. He asked Ed to make one of his nominating speeches at the convention. Ed hesitated, but Frank explained that his staff would write the speech for him. Ed would talk about the glory of America and the importance of protecting basic American industries from foreign competition. How Frank's economic policies would lead to prosperity for all, just as it had for Stellar's workers and the citizens of Star. It didn't seem too difficult. Ed said yes.

The night before his plane was due to leave for the convention in Los Angeles, Ed Johnson tossed and turned in bed, unable to sleep. He had practiced his speech. His wife and kids were healthy and asleep on a night in July in Illinois. His workers had never fared better. Stellar televisions were selling for $300 but his workers earned up to $200 a week. Only a week and a half to earn a television. The plant was at full capacity and there had been talk of expanding. What was bothering Ed Johnson?

At 2:00 A.M. Ed headed downstairs for a glass of milk and a piece of chocolate cake. He went back upstairs to the den, talking to himself. He walked over to the hi-fi, put on Frank Sinatra's *Only the Lonely*, and placed the needle on the mournful "One for My Baby."

"Never did like government," he muttered. "I admit that quota bill sure has been good for Stellar Television. But I'm worried about a bill that would limit all foreign imports. Televisions are different. Electronics are the future of America. But all products? Maybe it won't turn out so well."

That was my cue. So while Ed was pacing the room, I got the Magistrate to approve my request to come back to earth for a night. Then I popped into the leather armchair in the corner. Ed didn't see me at first; he was too busy digging a trench in the carpet. When I finally caught his eye, he came to a full stop and gave out a snort of breath. His words of greeting were a nervous staccato.

"Whoa, my friend, who the hell are you?"

I had not heard much profanity from Ed Johnson in all the years I had observed him. Arriving unannounced in a man's den at two in the morning will jar even the most peaceful spirit.

"My name is David, but you can call me Dave. I'm—"

"Look here, Dave," said Ed gently, "are you hungry? There's fried chicken downstairs. How about a piece?"

Ed had taken me for a beggar of some kind looking for a warm place to stay and a meal. No call to the authorities. Just an offer of help.

"Thank you kindly, Mr. Johnson. I wish I could accept your offer, I truly do. Where I come from, we don't get hungry."

"Plenty to eat where you come from, then?" asked Ed in a nervous voice. The temperature had fallen in the room and Ed began checking the windows while he was talking, looking for a draft.

"The windows are all fine, Mr. Johnson. That draft you're feeling is my doing, I'm afraid. It's a natural consequence when a Wanderer touches down."

"A wanderer?"

"Yes. Mr. Johnson, have you ever seen *It's a Wonderful Life*?"

"Of course. See it every Christmas. One of my favorite movies."

"You remember Clarence in that film?"

"Sure. Clarence was George Bailey's guardian angel. Great how he got his wings in the end. Now, Dave, let's head downstairs. I'm sure there's something in the icebox to interest you."

"I'm afraid it doesn't quite work that way."

"What doesn't work what way?"

"Getting the wings. Mr. Capra was merely being fanciful."

"Is that so?" Ed reached for the telephone on his desk. "Why won't this phone work?" Ed asked, speaking to himself.

"Probably my doing, though I daresay I can't explain it. More in your line of work I would venture. Electricity, televisions—"

"Listen, Mister David whatever your last name is—"

"Ricardo."

"Listen, Mr. Ricardo, if you've cut my phone line I am going to lose my sense of humor—"

"Calm down, Mr. Johnson. Remember in *It's a Wonderful Life* how Clarence proves he's an angel? I just have to do something similar for you."

"Why don't you tell me why I'm eating milk and chocolate cake."

"Not too difficult. When you were a boy you used to go downstairs with your father on the pretext of making sure the lights were out. He would give you a glass of milk and a piece of chocolate cake. You and Steven have continued the ritual, but tonight, it is too late for Steven."

Ed sat down. I'd gotten his attention.

"Parlor tricks are so demeaning, Ed. May I call you Ed? I know you very well, far better than one who would know about the scar on your knee from that nasty fall as a child. Such knowledge does not establish my unearthly origins—a man with enough nerve and gumption could uncover such a detail. No, Ed, my ear is more finely tuned than you can imagine. I know of your dreams for your son Steven, and how you yearn to see your daughter Susan safe and secure. I too had such dreams for my children. I know your uneasiness at the thought of your alliance with Mr. Bates. You tossed and turned in bed tonight because of guilt, wasn't it? Guilt at knowing you had turned to others for help, that you sought unfair advantage for your company..."

Ed Johnson's gaze had softened and I knew I had struck home.

"Patience, Ed. You'll have real cause for guilt before the night is through. But you will have a chance for redemption that few men are given."

"I am at your service."

"We are going traveling in time. I am going to show you what will become of America if Frank Bates fails in his bid for the Presidency. If Frank Bates becomes President of the United States, America will become increasingly protectionist. Instead, I am going to show you the America of increasingly free trade. Perhaps when you see such a world, you will no longer support Frank Bates, and you will throw away that speech on your night table."

"I'm ready, Mr. Ricardo."

"Call me Dave."

"You don't have relatives in Cuba by any chance?"

"Cuba? I don't think so. Most of my relatives remain in England."

"The phrase 'Babaloo' doesn't mean anything to you then?"

"Ah, I catch the allusion. Very good, Ed. But I am afraid that is another Ricardo. No relation."

On that note, we soared into the future.

CHAPTER THREE

The Roundabout Way to Wealth

I chose the year 1995, to play it safe. That would give Ed enough of a taste of a world where Americans were free to trade with foreigners.

"Where are we?" asked Ed.

"My friend, we are in the parking lot of a movie theater in your hometown of Star Illinois, in 1995."

"Why would a movie theater need such a large parking lot?"

"There are eight theaters here and they need a lot of space."

"Eight theaters! What happened to the Bijou?"

"The Bijou, downtown? I'm afraid it was torn down in the name of something called 'urban renewal.' "

"That's too bad. Can we see the Stellar Television factory?"

"I'm afraid it's gone, Ed."

"Gone!" cried Ed, leaning against a Honda Accord for emotional support.

"I'm afraid so. In fact, this multiplex, the modern name for a collection of theaters, stands on the very spot where your plant once stood."

"I'll be damned, why—"

"Ed, watch your language. You may get your wish."

"Sorry. Is anyone making televisions in the United States anymore?"

"They are. In fact they're doing it with lower labor and raw material costs than you did in your best year."

"Must be Motorola. They always gave me a good fight."

"Motorola made its last television in 1974."

"Then who is it?"

"I'll show you. We'll have to leave Star for a bit. But that shouldn't be any problem for the people Upstairs."

"Where are we now, Dave?"

"Rahway, New Jersey."

"Where's the television factory?"

"You're looking at it."

"But the sign says 'Merck and Co., Inc., A Pharmaceutical Company.' Doesn't that mean they make drugs?"

"Indeed they do, Ed. They send some of those drugs to Japan. In return, Japan sends America televisions. There are two ways to make a television set—the direct way, and the roundabout way. The direct way is to build a factory like yours in Star and combine raw materials with people and machines to produce televisions. With the roundabout way of making televisions, you make televisions by making something else, such as drugs, and trading the drugs for televisions. Japan's drug industry isn't able to efficiently supply all of Japan's demand for drugs, so Japan imports drugs and exports televisions. What you see appears to be a drug manufacturer. But they also produce televisions for Americans to enjoy by exporting some of their production."

"But Merck doesn't send drugs to Japan for televisions. They send drugs to Japan for money."

"That is how matters appear. But Merck accepts Japanese currency for their drugs only because some American wants to use that currency to buy something from Japan such as televisions. If no one wanted to buy Japanese products, then Merck would have to use that currency as wallpaper. They wouldn't sell drugs to Japan."

"Couldn't they exchange the yen for dollars at a bank?"

"They can, as matters turn out. But matters turn out that way only because someone with dollars wants to buy something made in Japan and needs yen to do it. Otherwise no one would give up dollars for yen and the bank would not be in the business of currency exchange. You see Americans buying televisions and giving the Japanese dollars. And Japanese buying drugs with yen. But actually, Americans are swapping drugs for televisions. The currencies merely facilitate the transaction."

Ed looked at me warily.

"What happens when Japan increases its supply of domestically produced drugs?"

"Maybe they will or maybe they won't. Japan can't make everything. Well, they can, but they can't make everything equally well. Like every nation, their resources are limited. By their resources I don't mean just raw materials. I mean their people and the number of hours in a day, and how hard people wish to work. It's impossible for Japan to make everything better than anyone else in the world. And even if they could, it wouldn't be wise for them to do so."

"Why not?"

"Even if they could, they would do even better by specializing in a few things rather than trying to do everything. Take yourself. I know you won the typing contest at Star High your senior year. Set the all-time record, didn't you?"

"I did."

"Yet as President of Stellar Television, don't you have your own secretary?"

"Of course."

"But you are a better typist than she is. Why did you hire her?"

"Because my time is better spent running the plant."

"Exactly. Your time is scarce. So even though you type much more quickly than Miss Evers, it would be stupid for you to do the typing. The same is true of Japan. As a nation, they specialize in producing televisions and import drugs even though they could train their television engineers to be chemists. America, in turn, wants both life-saving drugs and televisions. It produces both in the most efficient way possible, by making drugs, keeping some for domestic consumption, and sending the rest to Japan for televisions."

"Does this insight have a name?"

"It does, but it is not so catchy: The Theory of Comparative Advantage. A British economist figured it out."

"Who was that economist, Dave?"

"I cannot say I remember, Ed. At any rate, you and I will give it a different name: The Roundabout Way to Wealth. For the original name misleads. The 'comparative' in the title doesn't mean compared to other nations. It means compared to other products. Even though the United States excels at television production, Americans are even better at making pharmaceuticals. The United States has a comparative advantage not in televisions, but in pharmaceuticals, even though it might take less labor to produce a television in the United States than it does in Japan. The United States specializes in producing drugs and gives up making televisions. Just like you gave up typing to concentrate on managing your factory."

"But how do you know the roundabout way is cheaper? It's just a theory. The government stands back and lets Motorola and Stellar go out of business—"

"Motorola is still in business, Ed."

"But you said—"

"I said they stopped making televisions."

"OK, they stopped making televisions. So America makes televisions in the roundabout way. But Americans are sending money to Japan. Lots of money, I bet. Wouldn't it be better for the United States if that money stayed in America? That way, Americans have the money instead of the Japanese. With more money, we're richer. Isn't that better than sharing the money with foreigners?"

"It depends, Ed. The wealth of a society isn't measured by how many pieces of paper its citizens hold. If America does not trade with Japan, Ed, Americans have more pieces of paper. But do they have more goods and services and the leisure to enjoy them? Unless the Japanese send televisions to America out of the goodness of their hearts, then America has no Japanese televisions. Without Japanese televisions, America must make those televisions domestically. Making those televisions domestically requires people and raw materials. But the roundabout way of making televisions by making drugs and swapping them for televisions produces televisions more cheaply."

"The theory sounds pretty good, but how about some evidence? You claim that Merck can make televisions more cheaply using the roundabout way than I did with an old-fashioned television factory. Prove to me that televisions have gotten cheaper. And without using some fancy theory."

"Take it easy, Ed. Calm down. Back in 1960, how many hours did one of your workers have to work in order to earn enough money to buy a television set?"

"About two weeks."

"Today the average American has to work about 3 days."

"You're kidding! But what about the quality? If you're going to compare a 1960s television to one made in 1995, you've got to compare televisions of the same quality. If those televisions are made in Japan, they couldn't be very good."

"I'll let you be the judge of that. Let's go back to Illinois and take a look."

"I suppose Willie's Appliance Store is gone."

"I'm afraid so. Replaced by a frozen yogurt stand, a phenomenon we can explore later. But don't worry, you can still buy a television in Star."

Back in Star, I took Ed to a Circuit City to look at the televisions of the 1990s. He was overwhelmed by the array of shapes and sizes. We went over to a 20" color model.

"Ha!" said Ed. "$290! That's no bargain. You said the average worker could buy one of these in 3 days."

"The average worker can. Television prices are higher now than they were in 1960, but because of inflation, so is everything else, including wages. That's why it's useful to think about how many days of work it takes a worker to earn a television—it gets rid of the effects of inflation on both wages and the price of televisions."

"Three days. Amazing. And the sharpness of the picture is astounding."

"And unlike the older sets you are used to, Ed, these new models hardly ever break."

"As nice as these new televisions are, Dave, I can't believe America can't compete and make a product that is just as good. What happened to good old American know-how?"

"It's still functioning. It just got redirected to other more productive areas. It's like your typing skills—how could you give up typing when you were the best typist in the building? It was too costly for you to be your own typist. The gains to the factory from your superlative typing are less than the gains to the factory from your time spent managing the factory. It is the same with televisions. America could easily make the best televisions in the world."

"Then why don't we?"

"Because the resources it would take to make the best televisions are better spent making the best drugs and swapping them for televisions that other countries make."

"Maybe you're right, but how do you know? Who makes the decision not to specialize in televisions and to specialize in drugs instead? How do you know it's the right decision?"

"No one person makes that decision. That is what is hard to understand, but it's really rather beautiful. If some American could make the same quality television as the Japanese but at a lower cost, they could become fabulously wealthy. Evidently, a better American-made television would cost more to make than the current Japanese televisions."

"How do you know?"

"If it could be done, someone would make such a television and become wealthy. To make such a television you would have to pull engineers and manufacturing know-how out of other industries such as aerospace and computers and pharmaceuticals. The talent is better used in those industries."

"How do you know?"

"If it were not true, a television manufacturer could outbid those industries for the talent. Of course, a television manufacturer can always outbid those industries for the talent by paying a higher wage. But we do not see such a phenomenon occurring. Evidently the wage necessary to draw skilled labor out of other industries and into televisions is so large, an American television cannot be sold at a price that is competitive with the Japanese price.

"It's a little bit like the Olympics, Ed. In the 1970s and the 1980s, the East Germans and the Cubans dominated the Summer Olympics, particularly relative to their population. Americans wondered how such small countries could produce such great athletes. Americans were outraged. They clamored for a better Olympic team. Of course, America could win the gold medal in every Olympic event if it wanted to. America could mobilize a larger portion of her resources for training facilities and make sure that the best sprinters and high-jumpers and gymnasts pursued their craft full-time. A committee of experts would be appointed. They would take people not just from sports but people from all walks of life who had the potential to be athletes. The committee would make sure that these athletes were rewarded sufficiently to get them to be athletes instead of whatever else they were pursuing.

"America could win every gold medal that way. But would it be worth it? America would have some glory. What would go unseen are the activities and opportunities that were sacrificed to have the glory. It wouldn't be worth it. It wasn't worth it for East Germany or Cuba. Oh, the athletes involved lived pretty well. It was worth it for them. But while they were winning gold medals, the people of Havana and East Berlin were living in poverty and squalor. The free market would never have produced such outcomes. It took an authoritarian government to make a colossal blunder like that.

"A lesser but similar mistake would be to insist that America at least win the gold medal in the 100-meter dash because Americans have always won the 100-meter dash. Should America insist on making the best televisions in the world simply because you always have? If televisions can be made at a lower cost by the roundabout way, then America is better off producing them the roundabout way."

CHAPTER FOUR

Is Japan Winning the Economic War?

"While we're talking about the Olympics, Dave, if the Japanese are making large numbers of televisions, are they ahead of the United States?"

"Why would you care if America is ahead or behind?"

"But surely it is better to be ahead than behind?"

"Maybe. It depends on the nature of the contest and how you keep score. In the 1990s people often thought the Japanese were ahead if you looked at Japanese incomes converted from yen to dollars. But Japanese have to pay prices in yen. When you took account of the prices in Japan and what Japanese incomes could buy, the average American still had a higher standard of living than the average Japanese by about 25% in 1992."

"That's a lot closer than they were in 1960, I bet."

"You are right."

"Did they narrow the gap by dragging America down, or by improving themselves?"

"Some workers were harmed by Japanese competition between 1960 and today. But overall, America got wealthier. A lot wealthier."

"Can you prove it, Dave?"

"I would start with the evidence of your senses. The array of goods in that Circuit City store was pretty impressive, wasn't it?"

"Yes, it was. There was nothing like that back in 1960. Somebody must be buying those appliances and televisions."

"You could also look at your children and your worker's children and see that their standard of living is much higher than your generation's. But you don't know whether they are typical or not. To know what has happened to America overall you must look at wages or income for most or all of the population."

"What do you find?"

"The government collects data for what it calls 'production or non-supervisory workers.' They make up about 80% of the work force. In 1960, the average worker in this group made $2.09 per hour. In 1990, the figure was $10.02 per hour."

"But what about inflation?"

"Good point, Ed. After taking account of higher prices, the seeming fivefold increase in wages was in fact only 19%."

"Hmm. That's not a very impressive increase over 30 years."

"I agree. But there is a very misleading aspect of the comparison. In 1990, workers took much more of their income in the form of fringe benefits such as pension plans, health and dental insurance, and longer vacations. In fact, such forms of compensation more than doubled between 1960 and 1990. The right measure of a worker's well-being should measure all forms of compensation, not just hourly wages."

"What happens when you account for the increase in fringe benefits?"

"Hourly compensation increased by more than 60%."

"Quite impressive. America did get wealthier. So how did the gap narrow so much between the United States and Japan?"

"Japan grew even faster than the United States. Japan did exceptionally well between 1960 and 1990."

"But if the Japanese had stayed poor, America would have become even richer."

"Only if there were a fixed amount of wealth in the world and the nations of the world tussled over it. Again, the Olympic metaphor is misleading. Somehow, if Japan wins the gold medal in television production, America has somehow lost. In fact, their expertise and success frees up resources for America to specialize in other areas. Both countries are better off. But that didn't stop people from worrying about Japan."

"If both countries were gaining, why were people worried?"

"They believed in the Olympic metaphor where winning the gold medal means that someone else must lose it. They saw economics as war. They believed that Japanese policies enriched Japan at the expense of America. The most frequent complaint was unfair competition. People accused Japan of dumping."

"What's dumping?"

"Dumping is selling below cost."

"Why would a manufacturer sell below cost?"

"Because they make up the difference on volume. Sorry. That was a tired joke even 150 years ago. A good question. Why would a seller sell at a loss? The standard answer would be to penetrate the American market, weaken or destroy American competition, and use that leverage to exploit American consumers by raising prices."

"But that doesn't make sense, Dave. After they penetrate the American market, they will have to increase the price well above the original level to make up for their losses. This will alienate consumers. American producers, even if they couldn't afford to match the price cuts of the earlier period, would now find it profitable to re-enter the market. With prices back at their original level, the Japanese will not be able to recoup their earlier losses. The strategy looks disastrous."

"Bravo, Ed, bravo! Your logic is impeccable. But here is an alternative argument. Suppose the Japanese lower price below cost and force the American firms to match the price cuts. If the Japanese firm is patient, they can drive the American firm out of business. If it is very costly to shut down a plant and re-open it, then the American firm may choose to shut down for good rather than be part of a cycle of leaving and entering."

"But they don't have to shut down, Dave. All they have to do is refuse to match the initial price cuts of the Japanese."

"But who will buy from them if they have higher prices, Ed?"

"It depends. If no one buys from the American firm, then the Japanese find themselves serving the entire American market at a price at which they are losing money. They not only have to absorb the production of the American company, they have to make even more than this because they have stimulated demand with their lower price. This would surely be a back-breaker. To avoid these enormous losses, the Japanese company would have to limit the number they are willing to sell at the low price. This allows the American firm to still make sales and profits at its old price."

"Again I applaud you, Ed. Unfortunately your logic failed to convince everyone. Ultimately it came down to an empirical question. Did Japanese companies who were accused of dumping eventually succeed in raising price?"

"Well?"

"A number of industries came to be dominated by the Japanese through lower prices. American firms went out of business or turned to other products. But the prices stayed low, even when American competition disappeared. All kinds of consumer products that were made overseas such as watches, calculators, and cameras became inexpensive and stayed that way. The televisions we saw at Circuit City are a perfect example. Japanese firms accused of dumping seemed to leave price perpetually at a level that was allegedly below cost."

"But that's impossible!"

"Correct. Either the Japanese were not dumping in the first place or they were altruistic. They were selling products to the American consumer at below cost. Seems unlikely."

"But if they weren't dumping what was going on?"

"Can't you see?"

"They must have had a cost advantage of some sort."

"Exactly."

"I can think of two kinds of cost advantages, Dave. One is that they were better than we were at making televisions or some other product. But the second advantage would be an unfair one. Maybe their government was subsidizing their production."

"This was a common claim, advanced by the American producers who were trying to compete. But their argument was mostly irrelevant. Let's take the extreme case where the Japanese government subsidizes televisions or cars so heavily that the Japanese *give them away* to the American people. Can you think of a greater boon for a nation than to have a foreign nation using its scarce capital and labor to produce your goods for you without charging for them? That would be a wonderful world for America."

"But, Dave, what if the Japanese government gives the Japanese producers a subsidy, drives the American producers into bankruptcy, and then bang! It takes away the subsidy, and all of a sudden we're at their mercy. We have already closed down our car or television factories and the Japanese can jack up the prices."

"That argument sounds a lot like one you just rejected."

"I rejected the argument that a foreign company would incur enormous short-run losses, recoup those losses by charging much higher prices in the future, while hoping that American firms wouldn't re-enter the market. But in the case of a government subsidy, the government absorbs the losses. The Japanese firm doesn't have to worry about the losses when considering cutting price."

"Let's look at the issue from the other side of the Pacific. The Japanese eat a lot of rice. But rice in Japan typically costs five times more than rice in the United States. Do you know why?"

"Higher quality?"

"That's what the Japanese rice producer argues while arguing for a law that keeps out imported rice. It is this restriction on supply that keeps the price in Japan above the price in the United States. Suppose Japan were to allow United States rice into Japan, and suppose, for argument's sake, American farmers can supply *all* of Japan's rice needs at a price such that Japanese farmers do not find it profitable to grow rice. What do you think would happen?"

"Japan would destroy its rice fields and the United States would have a monopoly. They could raise the price and take advantage of Japan. The rice fields would be paved over and probably have office buildings on them. How could Japan start up those fields again? They couldn't—it would be too costly. Plus even if they did try to start from scratch, how would they know the United States wouldn't drop prices again and make them lose a lot of money. If I were a Japanese rice lover, I'd be plenty scared."

"Tell me, Ed. Where do you buy the wood for the cabinets of your televisions?"

"A lumber supply company outside of Chicago."

"Do you ever worry that they would double the price they charged you or even increase it 25% overnight?"

"No."

"Why not?"

"The guy knows I'd take my business elsewhere."

"How do you know that a new supplier won't try to charge the same inflated price your old supplier wanted to charge."

"I'd just say no and call someone else. Besides, the new guy would want my business. If anything, he'd give me a price cut to start using him."

"Don't you think that the same force of competition among suppliers would prevent American rice growers from exploiting the Japanese once the Japanese became 'dependent' on United States rice? There are lots of rice farmers in the United States who would be competing for Japanese customers. But even if the United States government took over the rice market and tried to run it as a giant monopoly to exploit Japan, the Japanese could still turn to suppliers in other countries. So unless rice grows only in a handful of places, the Japanese would have nothing to worry about."

"Then why does Japan keep out American rice?"

"And why would an American television manufacturer try to keep out Japanese televisions? Oh, he would certainly talk about protecting the American consumer from inferior foreign products, but that would not be the real story, now would it?"

"OK, OK. I see the point. Dumping is unlikely to be a profitable strategy. You're saying that American firms went out of business because Japan could produce the goods more cheaply. Competition among Japanese firms and those from other countries kept prices low. Both Japan and the United States were made better off."

"That's right, Ed. Japan didn't impoverish the United States by selling goods cheaply in the American market. The critics of Japan tried another argument, however—Japan enriched itself at American expense by not letting American firms sell their goods in Japan."

"Was it true, Dave? According to the roundabout way to wealth, if Japan keeps out American products, Japan has to make everything for herself and will lose the benefits of specialization. That should make Japan poor, not rich."

"Perhaps we will discuss it in more detail if we have time. But the basic facts suggested the opposite. The Japanese were never stupid enough to keep out foreign products. After all, Japan is a small island. In 1992, the amount the average Japanese citizen imported was not much different from the amount the average American imported—about $1,900 vs. $2,200."

"But that's from all other countries, Dave. Maybe the Japanese treated American goods differently, got an advantage over a major competitor, and harmed America?"

"Let's look at the numbers. In 1992 the average American imported about $430 worth of goods and services from Japan. Meanwhile, the average Japanese citizen imported about $580 worth of American goods and services. This type of statistic was conveniently ignored by American producers arguing for their own trade protection. They focused on the overall trade deficit with Japan—since there are about twice as many Americans as Japanese, a small per capita difference becomes a large overall deficit. But a lot of American products were selling in Japan."

"But what kind of products were they, Dave?"

"Japan's critics in America would argue that Japan only imported food from the United States and not manufacturing goods. The claim was that Japan was trying to reduce America to the status of a third-world country. In fact, in 1992, Japan's top imports from the United States were airplanes, computers, and electrical machinery."

"What else worried Americans about Japan?"

"In the 1980s and 1990s, Japanese companies bought a lot of American assets—American companies and real estate. People found such purchases alarming. They were afraid the Japanese would be able to manipulate these assets to harm Americans or steal the profits. For example, the Japanese bought the Algonquin Hotel in New York. It was something of a cultural landmark because a group of intellectuals of the 1930s used to gather there for a drink and try to impress each other with witty remarks."

"And what did the Japanese do with the hotel?"

"They tore it down and left an eyesore in midtown Manhattan to punish the American people and reduce real-estate values in the surrounding area."

"Aha!"

"Just kidding, Ed. Strangely enough, after paying an enormous sum for the property, they wanted to run it as profitably as possible. They did not turn it into the world's largest sushi restaurant or—"

"What's sushi?"

"Raw fish."

"Thank goodness for that decision."

"People were afraid they would create a super-modern high-tech hotel that would appeal to Japanese tastes. Instead they decided to restore the hotel to its grandeur of the 1930s. That was the most profitable use of the asset."

"I can see why people were worried about Japanese purchases of American assets. The Japanese earn all of the profits instead of the Americans who owned it before."

"That appears to be the case. But the exact opposite turns out to be true."

"Come on, Dave. If the Japanese own it, they get the profits. What could be more straightforward than that?"

"I don't know, Ed. I would have thought that after a few lessons in the roundabout way that you would be wary of 'straightforward' reasoning."

"I may not be used to roundabout reasoning, but I am getting used to being wrong. Let's hear it."

"Suppose you had a money tree."

"A money tree?"

"Yes, a tree that every year produced a beautiful harvest of money. If it will make the example easier to understand, think of an apple tree. After all, an apple tree is a money tree; you just have to go to the trouble of selling the fruit in order to turn it into money."

"OK."

"So you have a money tree. A twenty dollar bill tree. Every year this money tree has about five twenty dollar bills that ripen on it, for a total of $100. Of course, some years it rains more than other years and you get six bills. In the bad years you might get four. But on average, five bills for a total of $100. One day you decide to sell the tree. What would your asking price be?"

"I don't know, Dave. I don't know much about the money tree market."

"But you do. Let's reverse your position. Suppose you wanted to buy such a tree. How much would you be willing to pay for it?"

"Does the tree live and grow forever?"

"An excellent question. Let us suppose the tree lives for ten years and dies."

"Then I suppose the most I would pay for it would be $1,000."

"Why?"

"If the tree produces $100 per year for ten years, that's $1,000. If I could buy the tree for less than $1,000 I would make a profit. I would never pay more than $1,000 unless I liked looking at money trees."

"You are close to the right answer. You would certainly never pay more than $1,000. But if you think for another minute, you would not pay even close to $1,000. Your choice is to buy the tree or not buy the tree. Suppose the price is $1,000. If you do not buy the tree, you get to keep your $1,000. If you buy the tree, you can expect to earn $100 per year for ten years. Is $100 per year for ten years equal to $1,000?"

"No, I see that now."

"Why not?"

"One hundred dollars per year for ten years is worth less than $1,000. Rather than investing my $1,000 in the money tree, I could put it into a savings account and earn interest. At the end of ten years I would have my principal of $1,000 intact plus I would have earned a lot of interest along the way. So if the money tree is priced at $1,000, it is a bad buy."

"Exactly. A money tree such as the one I have described will have to sell for something less than $1,000. How much less depends on the rate of interest a person can expect to earn in alternative investments of equal risk."

"Fine. That is very interesting, Dave. But what does that have to do with the Algonquin Hotel?"

"Don't you see? The Algonquin Hotel, like every form of capital, is in its essence, a money tree. It provides a stream of income for a period of years, just like the tree. The selling price of such an asset depends on its future profitability. When an American puts the Algonquin up for sale, he will demand and be able to receive a price that is approximately equal to the sum of all the future profits of the hotel. It will actually be less than that because while the buyer waits to receive the future profits, the seller has invested the money and is receiving interest."

"Are you trying to tell me that when the Algonquin is making profits under Japanese ownership, that money is already in the pockets of the American who sold the hotel?"

"That's right. If there were no uncertainty, the profits earned by the new Japanese owners would be just canceled by the amount the American owners received when they sold the property plus the interest earned on the money in the meanwhile. Do you know what actually happened? Remember that the harvest of any money tree is in fact uncertain. In the 1980s, the Japanese paid a lot of money for a number of assets that were particularly renowned. They bought the Pebble Beach golf course and Rockefeller Center and other such properties. For better or worse, those properties turned out to be far less profitable than the selling price predicted. So the Japanese overpaid their American sellers. It looked like the Japanese were earning profits. In fact, on balance, the American sellers took money from the Japanese buyers."

"Why did the Japanese overestimate the future profits with such frequency?"

"Two answers come to mind. First, they happened to make a lot of purchases at a time when the real estate market was at its peak."

"Bad luck?"

"Bad luck. But the second answer is that they cared not only about the future profits. They were willing to pay a premium for some assets because they liked the idea of holding them. Just like someone might like looking at the money tree and be willing to pay over $1,000."

"Seems irrational."

"Hardly. Merely unprofitable in financial terms. When the pleasure of ownership is included, they still may have come out ahead. So it need not be irrational."

"Still, Dave, I can understand that some Americans disliked the idea of the Japanese owning Rockefeller Center. I once took Steven and Susan ice-skating there."

"I think the American selling Rockefeller Center was very eager to allow the highest bidder to be allowed to buy the property. The seller, an American, would not be sympathetic to the argument that a Japanese owner harms Americans. It certainly wouldn't harm the seller. And I ask you, Ed, would it really disturb you to skate at Rockefeller Center knowing that the ice was maintained by a foreigner?"

"I guess not."

"I should mention that when America raised the biggest outcry against Japanese ownership, in the 1980s, Japan was only the third largest investor in American assets, behind England and Holland. No one felt uncomfortable about Dutch purchases."

"So Japan didn't get rich by dumping their goods in America. They didn't get rich by keeping out foreign products. They didn't even get rich by buying American real estate. So how did they do it? Was it because they lost World War II and could start from scratch with all the newest technologies?"

"Hardly. How could it ever be a good idea to let somebody destroy your factory? If new technologies are superior to old, you can always junk your old factory and adopt the new technology."

"But wouldn't that be expensive? After all, you've already invested in the old technology. Why throw away that money?"

"Edward, Edward! Sunk costs are sunk. That money is already thrown away. Continuing to invest in the old technology won't bring back money that has already been spent in the past. That money is gone. The rational choice is between the costs and benefits of the new technology vs. the costs and benefits of the old technology from here on out. It costs the United States and Japan exactly the same amount to adopt new technology."

"Then what was the secret of Japanese success?"

"Some said it was the unique partnership between Japanese industry and its government. Japan had a government agency called MITI, the Ministry for International Trade and Industry, that many people credited with creating the Japanese miracle."

"Were they right?"

"MITI did back some winners with government funding and assistance. They also picked some losers. They tried to discourage Honda from going into automobiles and hampered Sony's success in electronics. Honda and Sony were eventually great successes. I believe that MITI's role was not critical to Japan's success; Japan also had great economic success in times when MITI did not exist or was insignificant."

"So, Dave, what was Japan's secret?"

"There was no secret. The road to wealth for a nation is quite simple. Use your resources wisely. By resources, I don't just mean the traditional natural resources of fertile land, oil, and minerals, but the know-how, education, ingenuity, and drive of the people. Using your resources wisely means giving the people the incentive to work hard and the incentives to innovate, to take risks."

"How did Japan do it?"

"The first part was education. Japan developed a serious universal education system for its children. It is too regimented for American tastes, but it is successful in Japan."

"And the working hard?"

"In that case, the war did play a part, in the same way the Great Depression affected the United States. In the 1980s there was a phenomenon called the Yuppie. Never mind how the name came about—a yuppie was a young person who pursued material well-being in an unseemly way. Yuppies were obsessed with having the best of everything. They saved little and spent much. Their lack of saving motivation was viewed as an indication of American decline.

"What people did not notice was that the yuppie was born in the 1950s. The parents of yuppies were born in the 1920s and 1930s. These parents, people like yourself, lived through the Depression. It changed them forever. They saw what the Depression did to people. They vowed to protect themselves from economic disaster. They worked hard and saved much. What is the most you have ever paid for a pair of shoes?"

"Twelve dollars."

"Yet in 1994 your son Steven paid $125."

"One hundred and twenty-five dollars? Why that's an outrage! How could he throw his money away like that?"

"Well, you do have to remember that all prices are higher in 1994 than they are in 1960. Yet even taking that into account, some wealthy people, young wealthy people, will spend more money on luxury items than their parents ever dreamed of in 1960. Children like Steven grew up differently than you did. Steven lived in a nicer house growing up than you did. His first house is many times nicer than your first house."

"But that sounds wonderful."

"In many ways it is. But Steven saves less than you did at the same age. The behavior of his generation makes people think America is in decline relative to Japan."

"Is it true?"

"No, Japan is just riding the wave a little bit later. America's economic devastation occurred in the 1930s with the Great Depression. Japan's occurred in the 1940s with World War II. By the 1990s, the Japanese children born at the end of the war will be in their 50s, at the peak of their careers. Because of what they saw their parents endure in the war, they have worked longer and harder. They've saved more. They are doing well. But their children, who are starting to enter the labor force in Japan, have grown up with a different experience. They will find hard work less appealing. They will find it harder to save their money than to spend it. By the 1990s, there will be articles in the Japanese press of the profligacy of the Japanese youth, just as there used to be such articles about American youth in the American press. Too much Nintendo, not enough calcu—"

"What's Nintendo?"

"A rather advanced form of pinball, a game you yourself probably played a bit of. The point is that the growth of the Japanese economy let America grow by using the roundabout way to wealth. And even if you believe comparisons are important and not the level of American well-being, it's going to get harder for Japan to continue to grow more quickly than the United States. As Japan gets wealthier, there are forces at work that slow the rate of growth. You can't extrapolate past success into the future indefinitely."

"If losing a war or undergoing a Depression spurs savings and work effort, are Japan and the United States the only successful countries?"

"They are not. West Germany, for example, did exceedingly well between 1945 and 1990. Despite the destruction to their economy from World War II, they have bounced back because they have a highly skilled, well-educated workforce willing to work hard."

"But what about East Germany, or even the Soviet Union? East Germany was not doing well in 1960. And even though the Soviet Union was on the winning side, they went through incredible devastation during World War II. Have they done well?"

"They have not. Unfortunately it is not enough to be smart and have the urge to work hard. A nation's laws and institutions must also give people the proper incentives to work hard. The communist nations have never given their people the incentive to work hard or take risks. If you work hard and yet make the same amount as your neighbor who is slothful, after a while you get tired of working hard. They also have devoted immense resources to bureaucracies working to control prices and wages."

"The inefficiency of communism seems obvious, Dave. Yet why do the communist nations keep using it?"

"They didn't. In 1989—"

"Yes?"

"Never mind, Ed. You may be able to accept an eight theater multiplex. You may stomach the idea of frozen yogurt. But if I told you what happens to the Soviet Union after 1989, you will call me a sham and a hoaxer and we will make no progress. You will just have to wait and see what happens for yourself."

CHAPTER FIVE

Do Imports Cost America Jobs?

"Everything you say about the roundabout way to wealth and the power of open markets makes sense, but what about unemployment? When we closed down our plant and Zenith and Motorola closed down theirs, America must have lost a lot of jobs."

"No. America just lost certain types of jobs. Do you like corn, Ed?"

"Yes, I do."

"Do you grow your own corn?"

"No."

"But you could, couldn't you? But you don't for the same reason you don't do your own typing. It looks like growing your own corn is incredibly cheap. You just have the cost of a little seed. But growing your own corn is in fact incredibly expensive because of the time it takes to weed and water and fertilize. That time appears to be free, but it is costly. You have lost the opportunity to work at some other activity, earning money, and using that money to buy corn. Or having the time for leisure. If you think of your household as a nation, you import corn. You produce it in the roundabout way just like America produces televisions."

"But what if I were really good at growing corn?"

"Even if you were a fabulous farmer, it *could* be cheaper for you to work at something else and buy corn instead of growing it. It depends on whether it takes fewer minutes to grow an ear directly, or earn enough money at some other job using the roundabout way. You could say that your household has 'lost' the corn-growing job. But this would be a silly way of looking at what has occurred. You have lost the job of growing corn and gained a more valuable opportunity."

"What does that have to do with the jobs in Star? Aren't they gone?"

"The television jobs are gone. But they have been replaced by others. Think about agriculture. Do you know what percentage of the American people worked in agriculture at the turn of the twentieth century? About 33%. Today that number is under 3%. In the case of agriculture, the number of people working in agriculture necessary to feed the American people has fallen dramatically not because of imports but because of increased technology. But did that technology cost America jobs? It cost America *certain types of jobs*, but the overall number of jobs has increased tremendously."

"But didn't those farming jobs disappear, Dave?"

"Not in the way you'd think. A farmer didn't wake up one morning to find his overalls gone, his tractor vanished, and his fields of grain replaced by a shopping center. As technology improved, some farmers' incomes fell. Some farmers retired early. Others sold their farms to more efficient farmers. And some just struggled until retirement. But the biggest change caused by that technology was invisible. The dreams of farmers' children changed. Those children saw that agriculture was not a booming industry. Even though their parents and grandparents had been farmers, they saw that farming was going to be less profitable than it had been in the past. They made plans to become salesmen, engineers, chemists, and pilots. The proportion of the workforce in farming has plummeted. But the jobs didn't disappear."

"You're saying that the people took different types of jobs."

"That's right. Some even went into a new industry called television. Can you imagine how poor America would be in 1960 or 1995 if it had tried to preserve the size of the farming industry in the name of saving jobs?"

"But the agriculture jobs we lost went to other Americans. It's not like we started importing food."

"What's the difference?"

"I don't know. It seems like the two cases ought to be different. When American farmers lost their jobs because other Americans figure out a new technology, at least the inventors who benefit are Americans. When American farmers lose their jobs because foreigners sell food to America more cheaply, the benefits go to foreigners."

"In fact, either way makes America better off."

"How?"

"In either case, America gets less expensive food with a smaller number of farmers. That is the important change. You see America losing jobs. I see Americans spending less on food—food is cheaper and fewer Americans have to work in the food business. This allows Americans to make more of other things instead of food. Let me ask you a question, Ed. Do you think it would be good for America if all disease disappeared and everyone were perfectly healthy until the age of 120?"

"Sure."

"Why do you answer so quickly? Aren't you worried about what would happen to the doctors? America would lose all those high-paying doctor and health care jobs."

"Oh come on, Dave. If we could get rid of disease, doctors shouldn't stand in the way. They would just have to find other things to do."

"And if America finds a cheaper way to make televisions by importing them?"

"It's just not the same. Cheaper televisions are not as important as getting rid of disease."

"But the principle is the same. Would a doctor have a right to force a person to stay sick so the doctor could continue earning the living the doctor was accustomed to? Does a television manufacturer have the right to force a consumer of televisions to pay a higher price for televisions to sustain high wages for his workers? But perhaps these are issues for a philosopher. In any case we don't lose jobs if we eliminate disease or if foreigners sell America inexpensive televisions. Certain *types* of jobs are lost. If disease disappeared, we'd lose the medical jobs. People who would have been doctors would now apply their skills to other activities and enrich our lives. Paradoxically, America would lose the high-paying jobs in health care but still become wealthier."

"And what about the people who are already doctors?"

"They would suffer hardship. The size of that hardship would depend on how disease disappeared. If it happened slowly, the hardship would be less and medical workers would have time to adjust. If it happened literally overnight, it would be a lot crueler. To the doctors anyway. The sick would rather see disease disappear quickly."

"Well, what about the automobile industry? That's even more important than television and electronics. The automobile industry connects the whole economy. I see a lot of foreign cars in this parking lot. How is the Ford plant down the road in Clarksville doing, and how about Jack Clements's car dealership here in downtown Star?"

"The Ford plant closed ten years ago. And Jack Clements closed his dealership and sold the land to the city. They turned it into a baseball field."

"OK, Dave. Here's your challenge. You tell me how a basic American industry like cars and the associated jobs like auto dealers can collapse like that and still make America better off. You can start by trying to convince me that Clarksville has the same number of jobs it had before that auto factory closed."

"It doesn't."

"But I thought the roundabout way of making cars through free trade preserved jobs—we didn't lose them."

"America didn't lose them, though Clarksville did. Between 1960 and 1990, the number of workers making cars for Chrysler, Ford, and General Motors declined by over 13%, from over 500,000 to under 450,000. Did America have fewer jobs? The overall number of jobs in the United States exploded between 1960 and 1990. In 1960 there were 66 million jobs in the

United States. By 1990 there were 117 million. So even though there were fewer jobs for people making cars, the overall number of jobs exploded."

"Wow. That is pretty impressive."

"Don't be misled. The ultimate reason jobs expanded was because the United States population was expanding and a higher percentage of that population, particularly women, wanted to work. But the key point is that there were jobs for that expanded population even though the Japanese and others were expanding into traditional American industries such as electronics, automobiles, and steel."

"So why did Clarksville lose jobs?"

"When they shut down that plant in Clarksville, there were fewer automobile jobs in Clarksville. Those auto workers were out of work. Some of them found other work in Clarksville. Some of them retired early. Some of them left Clarksville and went elsewhere. But overall, the number of workers in Clarksville fell. The new jobs that replaced the automotive jobs weren't in Clarksville. They were located elsewhere, nearer the workers with the skills for those new jobs."

"How does the roundabout way to wealth explain the poverty that must have followed? You can tell me that Merck is really a television company. And now that we've talked a little bit about the labor market, I understand what you were driving at. You were trying to tell me that the television jobs became higher paying pharmaceutical jobs. But what about the transition? My assembly line workers aren't chemists. When they lost their jobs, or the automobile workers lost their jobs in Clarksville, a drug company didn't spring up overnight and employ those people. They'd need new skills, new training. Some of them wouldn't be smart enough, or patient enough, to learn at their age. What happened to them?"

"Some of them suffered. But the biggest effect on Clarksville and on the families there was on the children of those auto workers. Just like fewer and fewer of the children of farmers over the last 60 years have looked for work in farming, the children of those Clarksville auto workers are not going to look to the automobile industry for their jobs or the direction of their education. Steel and machinery and human energy and skills are no longer being used to make automobiles. They're now free to go into other things—computers, airplane design, nursing, and so on. The children of the Clarksville auto workers will turn to those opportunities."

"But how do you know those opportunities will arise? It's all well and good to say that the automobile industry isn't a gold medal industry anymore, but how do you figure out what's going to replace it?"

"You can't. And no one has to. Self-interest will insure that opportunities arise."

"That doesn't reassure the worker and his children and his grandchildren. You're telling him, 'Don't worry. Your industry is disappearing, but something will come along some day and replace it.' I don't think he's going to find comfort there."

"It is not so much that something will come along and replace it. The children and grandchildren will turn their talents, whatever they may be, towards other industries."

"But what if there aren't any new industries?"

"I suppose that is possible. But it has never happened before. Imagine a farmer in 1910 worrying about the decline in farming. Suppose he knew that in 50 years there would be only a trivial number of jobs in farming relative to what there was in 1910. Sure he would be worried. But if he could see into the future and see the invention of the television and advanced farming techniques and the myriad of other activities of 1960, he wouldn't be worried at all."

"I don't know, Dave. You say the children benefit eventually, but it sounds pretty rough on the parents. They've lost their jobs, and their kids have moved on. Clarksville must be a ghost town."

"The town is not what it once was. And it is sad. To open up opportunities for others means hardship for some. Take Jack Clements and his Ford dealership here in Star."

"That car dealership was his life, Dave. You can't know what it meant to him. Selling that dealership must have broken his heart."

"It did."

"How can that be good?"

"It was not good for Jack. But think about Jack's son, Danny. Remember him? He was Steven's childhood friend."

"I know that family well. Jack always dreamed of having Danny take over the dealership and settling down here in Star."

"Sure that's what Jack wanted. But Danny had no dreams of running a car dealership. When Jack had to sell the place, Danny was free."

"That's ridiculous. Closing the auto dealership didn't set Danny free. If he didn't want to work for his father he didn't have to. He could always have done something else."

"Of course he could. But his options would not be the same. If the government commits to maintaining the size of the auto industry as a constant, that means fewer resources are available for other things. Remember the example of agriculture. Do you think Jack Clements would have run an auto dealership for half his life if the government back in 1900 had committed to keeping one third of the population in farming? It just couldn't happen."

"So where did Danny end up?"

"He works for Procter & Gamble in their finance department. Procter & Gamble is a typical American success story of the late twentieth century that no one notices."

"Why not?"

"Because it doesn't look like manufacturing, and it doesn't look like it uses fancy technology. In fact, it's quite sophisticated."

"What's sophisticated about selling laundry detergent?"

"In the 1980s, Procter & Gamble made the decision to become an international company. They sell their products all over the world. They try to make sure their products are the market leader, or at least the runner-up. Otherwise they get out of that product line. That requires constant innovation on the part of their engineers, their chemists, and their marketing people. In addition, when they have taken their products around the world, they have made sure that they were consistent with consumer demands."

"Do you think that's any consolation to Jack Clements?"

"Probably not, but it might be if he knew the connection between his hardship and the opportunities available to his son. He sees his dreams dying. He sees the labor of thirty years, embodied in his auto dealership, turning to nothingness. He feels like a failure. But he is not a failure. He had a run of thirty good years and provided people with their cars and excellent service. He sees that dealership as his child, but he does not understand the relationship between the dealership and his real child, Danny. The death of that dealership and the death of other economic ventures around the country are what gives kids like Danny the opportunity to pursue their dreams. Can Jack at the age of 55 retrain himself to pursue a new career? Some older workers can, but, sadly, Jack cannot. However, new careers are available to his son precisely because Jack's opportunities and the opportunities of others like Jack have changed so dramatically."

"But Jack wanted Danny to settle down in Clarksville."

"Danny won't now. Jack wanted Danny to run his dealership. He won't now. He wanted his dealership to be his legacy. It isn't. Danny is his true legacy. Is the life of Jack Clements a tragedy? I do not know. There is always an element of sadness when dreams are thwarted. But protecting Jack Clements and his dealership from failure thwarts the dreams of Danny Clements and the children of Americans who want the widest range of opportunity possible. To tell Jack Clements that his dealership cannot fail is to condemn Danny Clements to a static life of American-made products only, some first-rate, some indifferent, some poor. It is to close off boulevards of dreams for the Dannys of America because without change and success and failure, the world becomes less rich."

"Money isn't everything, Dave."

"You are right. When I say rich I don't just mean monetary wealth. I mean all the ways that life can be rich. Richness of experience and time. And monetary wealth does help a nation produce more walks on the beach and candle-lit dinners and health innovations that improve the quality as well as the quantity of life."

"What about my workers, Dave? What happened to the ones in Star?"

"The factory didn't shut down overnight. You struggled during the 1960s to compete with the Japanese. You finally sold your plants to the Japanese in 1975."

"I made a deal with the Japanese?"

"They made you a good offer and promised to keep your factories open."

"Did they keep their promise?"

"Not exactly. They closed the plant in Star in 1978, throwing 4,000 of your workers out of work. You had laid off the other 1,000 before they bought you out."

"I can't believe I trusted them to keep their promise."

"They tried, Ed. The television market turned sour at the end of 1970s. There was price pressure on the Japanese. They kept your factory outside of Chicago open. They still run it, in fact."

"That's some consolation, I suppose."

"Though they don't do much of the work there. It's mainly an assembly plant. They import most of the components from low-wage Asian countries."

"What happened to those 4,000 workers?"

"Some retired. Some started their own businesses using the profit-sharing plan Stellar had in place. Some of those businesses thrived, some failed. Some of your workers went to night school and became accountants and lawyers. About a year after your plant closed, a couple of other factories opened in Star because companies knew of your workers' skills. Some of your workers found work there."

"And what were the wages they offered?"

"They weren't as high as yours. You were the best employer in town. Your workers loved you and your company, even after you sold out and the Japanese took over. They had a reunion of your workers ten years after the plant closed and there was little bitterness. They remembered the picnics and the dinners and the good times. They had a lot of good memories."

"But their wages fell when they had to take new jobs?"

"They did. Perhaps more importantly, as time passed, their wages didn't keep up with the wages in the rest of the American economy. But that was because your workers' skills were simple ones. Some of them had never finished high school. Only a handful of your workers, mainly the engineers, had been to college. Your workers suffered and struggled just as those Clarksville workers struggled and suffered. But the children of your workers had different lives than their parents. They used to grow up working in the plant in high school, then moving into the plant full-time when they graduated or even before. But when your plant closed, they had to look elsewhere for their opportunities. America provided those opportunities and those children prospered."

"Speaking of children, Dave, can I see mine? Steven always wanted to be President of Stellar Television. What is he doing?"

"Your son got involved with computers."

"You're kidding. Computers! Man tried to sell me a computer once. I took the train up to Chicago and he showed me a warehouse as big as my factory back in Star. The computer took up the whole warehouse. I asked him what it would do. He said it would do my payroll and keep track of my inventory. When he told me the price I said no thanks. What a dead-end industry!"

"You are in for a surprise, then, and this time a pleasant one. Some-one figured out how to shrink a computer to fit on your desk with plenty of room to spare. And it is unimaginably faster and cheaper than the one you saw."

"You're making this up."

"I'm not. Let's go see one. I think you'll like it."

"Was my son the man who shrunk that monstrosity?"

"No, but he put his own stamp on the industry. You'll see."

---------------- CHAPTER SIX ----------------

The New Generation
of American Know-How

I took Ed to see his son. He lived in Palo Alto, California.

"Strange house, Dave. Where are we?"

"California."

"I can't say it's much bigger than my own. You said a lot of the children of my workers did better than their parents. Is Steven doing better than his old man?"

"Steven bought this house for $600,000."

"$600,000! You're kidding! It's a nice house, but no house is worth $600,000."

"Evidently it was. A lot of people want to live in California these days. It keeps the price of housing high. Let's see the den. I think you'll enjoy it."

We watched Justin, Ed's 15 year old grandson, do his homework. Ed was rather confused at first. Justin sat on the couch in front of a big screen television. A computer sat on a nearby desk. Justin would call out the name of a mathematical function, and a color three-dimensional representation would appear on the screen of the television.

"That is some screen, Dave. Who's working the controls?"

"Your grandson, Justin."

"How? Is there somebody behind the screen manipulating some knobs or dials?"

"No, Ed. The computer is able to recognize Justin's voice and respond to his commands. Your son Steven perfected the technology that makes it happen."

Ed didn't say anything, just swallowed hard. Justin asked his Dad if he could watch a video and his Dad said OK, as long as Justin didn't watch more than a few minutes. Had to watch his eyes, his Dad said.

"What's wrong with his eyes?" asked Ed.

"Don't worry. He's OK. There's a special medicine he takes. He's going to be fine."

"Where does Steven manufacture his computers?"

"Nearby. You'll find it ironic—he buys a lot of his parts from your old competitor, Motorola."

"Motorola?"

"When Motorola closed down their television assembly plants, they too turned to computers. But they make semiconductors—little pieces of machinery inside the computer that conduct information at unimaginable speed."

"What happened to their workers?"

"Much like what happened to those at Stellar. Some retired early, others moved on, some faced hardship with little or nothing to turn to. Some of them stayed on and learned how to design, make, and sell semiconductors. But you'll be surprised to know what happened overall. In 1960, Motorola had about 14,000 employees. But now Motorola employs 60,000 people in the United States making semiconductors and wireless communications systems—phones you can carry in your pocket wherever you go. And they've become an international company, like so many others. Worldwide, they employ over 100,000 people."

"So I guess you're trying to tell me that America didn't lose those Motorola television jobs. We replaced them with something better in semi-whatevers."

"Well, America didn't really *replace* the jobs, it's more that the people who would have taken those jobs instead did something more productive. But you've got the right idea. American creativity was unleashed to improve computers. Americans make the best computers and the best programs to make them work. In fact, Star now has a number of firms that assemble components for computers that your son buys. And some of your workers work in those companies."

I had trouble dragging Ed out of there. Between beaming at his grandkid and watching *Aladdin*, which Justin watched after finishing his homework, Ed was pretty comfortable in the den. I finally talked him into leaving. We still had to find Susan and the night was passing.

"Why, I bet Susan has three or four kids by now. I wonder what her husband does."

"I think you'll be more interested in what Susan does."

"Susan? She doesn't have to work for a living does she? Is her husband a bum?"

"No, but women have changed quite a bit over the last thirty-five years. In 1960, there were 21 million working women. By 1992, there were 53 million. This wasn't just due to population growth. The percentage of women who worked went from 35% to 54% over the same time period."

"How could they all find jobs? A lot of my workers are women. But most jobs for women are telephone operators, teachers, and nurses. How did they all find work?"

"That's the great thing about the labor market, Ed. As more and more women entered the work force, they didn't all want to be working at the traditional female jobs. They wanted to try other things. And those other opportunities opened up for them. The jobs weren't in the traditional American manufacturing areas such as steel and automobiles. They were in the new areas that expanded—entertainment, the pharmaceutical industry, and others. The biggest expansion was in service industries. In fact, Susan entered the retail trade industry."

"Retail? Is she selling make-up?"

"No, that would have been an uninteresting application of her MBA."

"MBA? Susan got an MBA?"

"Susan went back to school and got her MBA in 1985 from Washington University in St. Louis. She got interested in manufacturing. Took a job with Mast Industries, the manufacturing and import arm of The Limited, a chain of retail stores out of Columbus, Ohio."

"But retail is just buying something and reselling it. Can't be much money in that."

"You'd be surprised. It looks like buying and selling but it's really knowing what the customer wants and getting it into the customer's hands as quickly as possible. Retailers like The Limited go all over the world to find the goods the consumer wants and manufacture or import them. Susan makes trips to Italy and France to see what fashion ideas might interest Americans. Then she contracts with factories in Hong Kong, China, and Israel to make the goods as cheaply and quickly as possible. She visits those factories to monitor quality and delivery times."

"That sounds fascinating. Must be kind of tough on her family, though. Susan is married, isn't she?"

"You bet. Her traveling can be rough on both her and her family. But they make do. A 1995 family is a little different from a 1960 one."

"Sounds like it."

"Another American strength in the 1990s is information. New technologies using computers and different kinds of communications changed the world in undreamed of ways. Retailing has been completely transformed. Take a store like Wal-Mart."

"Never heard of 'em."

"They didn't exist in 1960, but now they're bigger than Sears."

"What is their secret?"

"They do many things exceptionally well. But one key is their control of information. Wal-Mart has a state-of-the-art communications system. A man in their headquarters in Bentonville, Arkansas, can look at a computer screen and tell how many ties have sold in the past week at a store in Florida."

"Impressive. What's the good of it?"

"Wal-Mart isn't the only one with that computer. The tie manufacturer in St. Louis who sells to Wal-Mart has the same information on his computer screen. Rather than waiting for the store in Florida to run out of ties, and processing a new order ready in six weeks, the tie manufacturer can get busy making the ties in advance, and making the ones that are the best sellers. The alternative is to hold large numbers of ties in inventory so that you don't run out. Very expensive. With the computer system, the consumer benefits in two ways. The consumer finds a wider array of merchandise available, and at a cheaper price."

"Why is the price cheaper? With all that equipment and computers, isn't the price going to have to go up?"

"Actually, it goes down. The computer equipment is expensive. But both Wal-Mart and the tie manufacturer save a huge amount of money on inventory costs. First, their carrying costs go down—because they have smaller inventories, they have less money tied up that could be earning money elsewhere. Second, they don't waste money manufacturing bunches of different ties to be ready for orders, only to find out that some of those ties aren't popular."

"How does the consumer benefit? It sounds like Wal-Mart and the tie manufacturer are the ones who get rich."

"It looks that way, but Wal-Mart isn't the only store with the idea. Wal-Mart must compete with other chains who are also looking for ways to cut costs and lower price. Wal-Mart would like to keep the profits from those cost savings, but competition forces them to pass much of the savings on to the consumer. Prices have fallen dramatically."

"What does this have to do with free trade and imports?"

"As America became part of the global economy and imports increased, service jobs expanded and manufacturing jobs contracted. A lot of people consider this change dangerous. They look at retailing, for example, in the way you do—buying something and reselling it. It seems inferior to manufacturing. What people have trouble seeing is that distribution and retailing and finding out what the consumer wants is just as important as making the good itself. Saving money on distribution the way Wal-Mart does is equivalent to finding a cheaper way of manufacturing ties."

"That's true, Dave. The customer doesn't care why the price is lower."

"But many people felt the way you did when you talked about the gold medal jobs. Service jobs sounded menial and second-rate in comparison to manufacturing jobs. People think of flipping hamburgers, earning the minimum wage in a fast-food restaurant. Some service jobs do pay poorly. But besides retailing, America has become world-class in many high-wage service industries that provide unique products better than anyone else in the world."

"For example?"

"The extremely innovative financial industry. As a one-time

financier in my youth, I find the complexity of today's financial instruments and how they are tailored to the demands of the customer extraordinary. Or take package delivery. A company called Federal Express changed
the way people thought about time and space. They guaranteed overnight
delivery anywhere in the United States."

"That must have been very costly to achieve, Dave. How could there
be a market for such a product at the prices they would have to charge to
make a profit?"

"When Federal Express got started, every package, even one going
from Seattle to San Francisco, went to Memphis, Tennessee, was sorted,
and then shipped to its final destination."

"But that's ludicrous. That can't have been a profitable way to do it."

"That's what all the experts said, even when Federal Express was a
booming success. The experts were wrong. The company made enormous
profits and established operations around the world."

"That's impressive, Dave. But it's hard to believe that retailing or
package delivery can be as valuable as the actual manufacturing. I understand how an economy isn't quite like the Olympics. But aren't automobile
and other manufacturing jobs worth a gold medal, while retailing and service jobs are second-rate? Aren't the manufacturing jobs the highest paying
jobs?"

"First, there is no gold medal industry, not manufacturing, and not
automobiles. The scarcity and productivity of the skill being used is more
important than the sector the job is in. In the 1990s, people who worried
about America losing manufacturing jobs kept talking about how important it was to 'make things' rather than provide services. Federal Express
doesn't make anything. But they employ almost 100,000 people at high
wages."

"But don't manufacturing jobs pay better?"

"In 1960, manufacturing workers made 12% more per hour than
other workers. Over time, manufacturing became increasingly mechanized.
The low-paying manufacturing jobs migrated to other countries. America
kept the higher-paying manufacturing jobs. Between 1960 and 1990, the
proportion of workers in manufacturing fell from 31% to 17%."

"And what happened to the pay for manufacturing jobs relative to
the rest of the economy?"

"In 1990, it was still about 10% above non-manufacturing wages."

"Why would you want to lose the jobs that still paid 10% more than
other jobs? You told me America has gotten wealthier between 1960 and
1990. But we would have been even wealthier if we had kept the proportion of manufacturing jobs at 31% or even higher."

"The exact opposite is the case. If America had kept those manufacturing jobs, America would have gotten poorer."

"How can that be?"

"Not all manufacturing jobs pay well. Between 1960 and 1990, the lower paying manufacturing jobs left America. It is precisely because the proportion fell from 31% to 17% that the wage premium for manufacturing stayed as high as 10%. If you had kept all the jobs in manufacturing, they wouldn't have paid so well. As time passed, workers on the assembly line weren't earning such high salaries. It was better to be one of the people inventing and producing the machines the workers on the line were using. Or doing something entirely different. When your plant finally closed, for example, your workers were earning well below the national average. The skills of your workers could not command a high wage anymore."

"Why did that happen?"

"Supply and demand. More people in more and more nations were able to build factories and fill them with workers smart and disciplined enough to work those factories. Part of that was due to increased education in those other countries, but a lot of it was caused by changes in the manufacturing process itself. As assembly jobs got more and more mechanized, it became easier and easier for low-skill workers to assemble products. That's one reason, along with technological innovation and competition, that televisions and watches and calculators got cheaper and cheaper, and stayed that way."

"Why, Dave?"

"Because the process of assembling those products required less skill. Those assembling jobs migrated from the United States to Japan to Taiwan to Hong Kong and continued to still lower-wage countries where the workers, though relatively unskilled, still had enough skills to assemble those products."

"Did the countries that were stealing jobs from America do well?"

"Now, Ed. They weren't stealing jobs from Americans. They were taking over the lower skilled jobs and freeing up Americans to find opportunities more consistent with their higher skill level. In fact, within those countries, the same thing was happening. In the 1970s, Hong Kong was a booming manufacturing area. But in the 1980s, Hong Kong lost manufacturing jobs and replaced them with service jobs, just as the United States did. In 1980, 46% of Hong Kong's labor force was in manufacturing. By 1991, that had fallen to 26%. Meanwhile, service jobs expanded from 35% to 60% of the labor force."

"What happened to those manufacturing jobs?"

"They emigrated to China and other countries with lower wages than Hong Kong. But Hong Kong got richer. In the decade of the 1980s, their real standard of living almost doubled, even though they had lost all of those 'gold medal' manufacturing jobs. If they had insisted on keeping them, Hong Kong would have become poorer. The same is true for the United States."

"Explain this to me, Dave. I can see why it is foolish for me to do my own typing in my factory. But what if the Japanese take all the management jobs and leave us with the typing? I can see that swapping manufacturing jobs for service jobs can be beneficial. But it can also be harmful. How do you know any of the good jobs will be left?"

"People worried about such matters when American companies failed to compete successfully with the Japanese in a particular industry. They feared that Japan would hoard all the good high-paying jobs. They even worried about a sinister plot of the Japanese government to target specific high-tech industries for Japanese success using subsidies. It was a variant of the dumping argument. The claim was that the Japanese government was willing to absorb losses not because Japanese companies eventually planned to raise prices. The goal instead was to capture the high wage jobs associated with high technology. Americans who feared this strategy would say, 'Remember, it's better to make computer chips than potato chips.' "

"Isn't it?"

"It depends. Some workers in the potato chip business make a good living. But the real flaw in the saying is the implication that if America gets pushed out of the computer business by unfair foreign competition, or even loses out in a fair fight, the only jobs that are left are the menial ones. But jobs aren't sitting there like boxes waiting for people to jump into them. Think back to the high-paying medical jobs that wouldn't exist if disease were eliminated. Do you think the people who would have been doctors are now going to be street sweepers? Or workers on an assembly line processing potato chips? They are not. They are going to take their skills and discipline to learn about something other than medicine. There is no limit to the human imagination. America's greatest resources are knowledge, know-how, and creativity. Such markets can never be cornered. There have always been occupations that use these skills and there always will be."

"OK, I give up. Dave, you're wearing me out. I need a break. Can we see Susan now?"

"Sure, but we have to do a little traveling."

We visited Susan's house in a suburb of Boston. Then we went over to a nearby park where Susan and her husband watched their daughter playing in a Little League game.

"Girls playing Little League, Dave?"

"I told you the 1990s were a little different from the 1960s."

"Why does the ball sound so funny?"

"It's not the ball—it's the bat. It's made of metal."

"Metal bats?"

"Some are even made in Japan. They never break. It keeps the cost down."

"I don't know what's harder to get used to—girls playing baseball or metal bats. But I'm mighty proud of my kids, Dave. They seem to thrive in a world of international trade. It makes up for a lot after losing the factory and the changes that Star has gone through. The future looks pretty good from the present. But I've still got my doubts. Star is real ugly. All those parking lots and big stores and hideous colors on all of the signs."

"The kids don't think so. To them it looks the way Star is supposed to look. If they were to be put in the Star of 1960, they would find it archaic and quite ugly in its own way."

"Even so, though I'm proud of how my children have turned out, maybe life would have been better for them without all of these changes. For one, Susan might still be living in Star with more than one kid. And what about all my workers who lost their jobs? Sure, my kids and some Americans prospered. I'll grant the possibility that America might be better off producing televisions in the roundabout way. But how about my workers? Some of them, maybe all of them, are worse off than they would have been. How do I know things might not have been better for them in a different world?"

Ed was loyal to his workers. I could see he was also still worried about Jack Clements and those Clarksville workers whose automobile factory went broke. I had an idea on how to give Ed more information, but it took an extension of my powers. I took Ed back to Star and over to where Willie's Appliance Store once stood, and bought him a frozen yogurt. It was not a big success. While he nursed it, I excused myself and ducked Upstairs to make a special request.

CHAPTER SEVEN

Do Tariffs Protect American Jobs?

"You know," said Ed, gazing down at what once was frozen yogurt, "this isn't that bad after all."

"You are eating what has become a vanilla ice cream cone."

"How could that happen? Hey, where are we?"

Ed and I stood on the corner of Main and Oak, downtown Star, Illinois, in 1995, in front of Willie's Appliance Store.

"Now this is the Star I know and love," beamed Ed.

"Are you sure?"

"At least it looks and feels right. The buildings look the way they used to back in 1960 and the stores are all there. One thing is bothering me, though. Why are so many people driving Ford Fairlanes and Chevy Impalas?"

"That's all everyone drives."

"What happened to Chrysler?"

"They went out of business in the early 1980s."

"Why? And why do Ford and Chevrolet offer such a narrow range of products?"

"People couldn't afford to buy as many cars as they once did. You see, Ed, this is how Star will be in 1995 if America has no imports. This is what America will look like if Frank Bates becomes President and his second bill passes. His first bill 'protected' Americans from foreign televisions. His second bill eliminated all imports and will stay in force permanently. What you see around you is a self-sufficient America. But without imports, America has to devote a lot of resources to make things they hadn't made before. Those items got so expensive, people could not afford the same cars as they did before. It all started with televisions. You got your bill passed—"

"It wasn't my bill, it was Frank Bates's bill."

"But you gave him the idea. When that bill passed, your company did exceedingly well. Sales went up, production went up. You hired more workers. To get them to leave their previous jobs and come work for you,

you increased the wages you paid. Star was booming and everybody could see it. There were new buildings going up all over town. Your workers were driving Cadillacs and Lincoln Continentals. Some were driving Corvettes. They dressed well. They built themselves fancier and fancier houses."

"So what was wrong with that? That sounds pretty good."

"It was. For your workers. But overall Americans were harmed."

"I disagree. Completely. First if someone gets richer, how does it hurt others? You told me earlier that when Japan got rich, it didn't hurt the United States."

"Getting rich doesn't *have to* impoverish someone else. But it can, as we shall see. Second?"

"Second. We've talked a lot about how we don't lose jobs when we import goods. If I understand the argument, we only lose those types of jobs. But you admitted that imports cause dislocation and hardship for some."

"In the short-run, yes. And I also admitted the short-run may not be so short for some people."

"Then it seems to me that a pretty good case can be made for restricting imports in some fashion. It prevents that short-run hardship."

"Without that hardship, there are no benefits to be enjoyed in the long-run. But more importantly, I am going to show you that you cannot avoid hardship by restricting imports. Let us start by examining the workings of a tariff on televisions."

"But Congressman Bates's bill wasn't a tariff. It just limited foreign imports. And it was for my workers' protection."

"I know, Ed. You asked for a quota. But it turns out that a tariff and a quota are virtually the same."

"How can that be? The tariff is a tax that applies only to foreign-made goods. But a quota doesn't force the foreign manufacturer to raise his price the way a tariff does. It merely limits what he can sell at the old price. It's much more fair."

"We shall see, Ed. Let us begin with a tariff. A tariff on imported televisions increases the price of both foreign and domestically produced televisions. It expands the market of American television producers and contracts the market for foreign-made televisions."

"Wait a minute, Dave. Why does it raise the price of domestic televisions? The tariff isn't on domestic televisions, just foreign ones."

"Funny, that's what every American automobile executive says when he asks for a tariff on foreign cars. 'We would never change our prices just because of a tariff.' Not surprisingly, this promise is always broken."

"Why? How can they raise prices when they don't have to pay the tax?"

"Let's stick with televisions. Suppose that before the tariff is imposed, domestic and foreign televisions with the same features and roughly equal quality are selling for $250. Now the American government imposes a tariff on foreign televisions of $25. A tariff is just a fancy word for a tax on goods made by foreigners. A $25 tariff means that every foreign seller who sells a television in the United States must pay $25 to the U.S. government."

"So he increases his price to $275 so he can make the $250 he made before."

"Not so fast. He would like to increase his price to $275. He would like it even better if he could increase his price to $300. But what a manufacturer would like to do and what he is able to do are not necessarily the same. Competition among suppliers constrains the power of the profit urge."

"But foreign televisions do get more expensive, don't they?"

"Yes, they do. Otherwise it won't be worthwhile for foreigners to bring televisions to America given that they have to pay a tariff in America. Let's not worry about the exact size of the price increase for now. When foreign-made televisions get more expensive, people who used to buy the foreign-made televisions will want instead to buy the American televisions of the same quality that are now cheaper in comparison. When more people want to buy something than before, the price goes up."

"But that's not fair, Dave! The American manufacturer hasn't been hit by a tax. He has no right to raise his price. His costs haven't changed."

"Perhaps it seems unfair. But consider the alternative. Suppose the American manufacturer does not increase his price. What will happen?"

"He will make the same amount per television as he made before. Seems fair."

"But if he makes the same amount per television as he made before, will he expand his output or keep it unchanged?"

"Keep it unchanged. You're not going to open a new factory and expand your capacity without a higher price. You would have already opened all the factories that would be profitable at the old price."

"Exactly. But while domestic television production is unchanged, Americans want to buy more domestic televisions than they did before because of the price increase of foreign-made televisions. Too many consumers are chasing too few televisions. What do you think is happening in the stores?"

"Customers are finding that the television they planned to buy is gone when they get to the store. Consumers will be lining up before the stores open to be sure to get the television they want to buy."

"So the true price of buying a television has already gone up. If the seller of American televisions does not raise the price on the televisions, the true price increases anyway because the buyer must now sacrifice time waiting in line to buy a television."

"I guess the seller would raise the price after all. Even at the higher price, he can sell the same number of televisions he sold before because his competition from abroad was hit with the tariff."

"Very good, Ed. In fact, even if the seller failed to notice the lines outside his shop, customers would drive prices higher by offering a higher price in order to avoid standing in line."

"OK, OK, so the price of both American and foreign televisions rises with a tariff."

"In fact, as you guessed, both prices will often rise by the full amount of the tariff, for reasons we need not explore. In our example, the $250 television has become a television selling for $275 whether it is made in America or abroad. American producers expand output in response to the increased demand for their product and the higher price. New American television factories are opened. The demand for workers with the skills to work in a television factory goes up. So do their wages."

"Sounds good for America. Higher wages and more jobs."

"It is good for *some* Americans. Your workers, for example, and your stockholders. The increase in the price of televisions makes them better off. Is anyone worse off?"

"I guess people who buy televisions have to pay more than they did before."

"Exactly. Some Americans continue to buy foreign televisions at the new price of $275. Others buy American-made televisions at the same price. The increase in price makes consumers of televisions worse off. What happens to the extra $25 they are now paying for televisions? The extra $25 paid to foreign suppliers gets recaptured by the American government in the form of tariff revenue. The extra $25 paid to American manufacturers increases their profits and the wages of their workers."

"Is that wrong, Dave? If the benefits in the form of tax revenue and higher profits and wages cancel the losses, it seems like a wash."

"On the surface it appears to be a wash. Of course it means that those Cadillacs and Lincolns your workers were buying with their higher wages were paid for out of the pocket of the American television consumer. Each consumer had to give up $25 worth of some good so that your workers could prosper. The gains to workers look larger because there are many fewer of them compared to the number of buyers of televisions. So while the loss by each consumer of televisions is only $25, the gain to each worker is much, much larger."

"I still don't see what's wrong with that."

"One could argue that it is a form of extortion. Your workers took money from the pockets of television buyers. How? Not by making a better product, not because there were not enough televisions to go around due to increases in your cost, but merely because the government restrained your competition. But that is a philosophical issue we perhaps should set aside. Surely you can see how the fancier cars your workers drove gave a false impression of a higher quality of life for Americans. You just don't see the poorer standard of living for the television buyers. Some Americans benefited, others lost."

"OK, OK. But some Americans are better off. Some are worse off. Maybe the gains to those who win are bigger than the losses to those who lose."

"Alas, in fact, the size of the losses outweigh the gains."

"How do you know, Dave?"

"Every television, imported or domestic, is $25 more expensive than it used to be. So every buyer of televisions has lost $25 relative to a world without the tariff."

"But, Dave, hasn't every producer gained that $25? It still seems like a wash."

"Not quite. The gain to the American producer is less than $25."

"Come on, Dave. How can a $25 loss not be somebody's $25 gain?"

"Paradoxical, isn't it? Here is why, Ed. If you did nothing in response to the higher price of televisions, then your profits on each television would indeed be $25 higher, and the losses of the consumer would be offset by your gain. But the increase in the price of television encourages you to make more televisions. You expand production at your existing plant, and perhaps build an additional one. But the costs of those additional televisions are not going to be the same as the costs of the smaller number you made before. The new televisions you make will be more costly. Your profits on the new televisions you make will be less than $25."

"Why?"

"Because you will not be able to run two factories as efficiently as one, for example. The manager you hire for the second plant will not be as skilled as the first, and you will not be able to keep an eye on two plants as well as you did when there was only one. As a result, your profits on those new televisions will be less than $25."

"But sometimes expanded production leads to *lower* costs. Haven't you heard of economies of scale, Dave?"

"I have kept up over the years, Ed. Yes, I have heard of economies of scale. But why would you wait for a tariff to expand your production and lower your costs? The wise manager will have already exhausted any available economies of scale. Additional expansion in response to a tariff will raise your costs. And that is why a tariff is not a wash for America as a whole. The harm to consumers is larger than the benefit to producers and their workers."

"How can that be, Dave? I still don't quite see how the losses and gains don't balance out."

"You have to remember how people respond to incentives. Your company responds to incentives by expanding production. That means more resources get devoted to televisions. That is not free. You use up more American resources in your bid for television sales that have gotten $25 more lucrative than they were before. America as a whole is poorer."

"Is that the end of the story?"

"No. Television manufacturers are not the only ones responding to incentives. Let us look at the chain of events again. The tax on foreign-made televisions increases the demand for American televisions and reduces the demand for foreign televisions. The price of American-made televisions also rises. American production expands, but imports have fallen. What happens to the total number of televisions bought by Americans? It falls, even though American production has gone up. The reduction in imports always outweighs the increase in production from American sources."

"Why?"

"Because the overall price of all televisions, domestic or foreign, has gone up. Nothing has happened to change the number of televisions people want to buy except an increase in price. When televisions are more expensive, people want to buy fewer televisions. Americans, taken as a whole, are worse off because they have fewer televisions to enjoy."

"Wait a minute, Dave. If Americans had fewer televisions, then they had more of something else. You're saying that while some Americans were harmed by the increase in price and lost $25, some stopped buying televisions entirely. But this means they had the $250 they used to spend on televisions left over to buy something else with. So they had more of something else."

"Quite right. But we know that whatever they buy with the $250 is not as valuable to them as the television was."

"How can you tell?"

"Let us say a man who used to buy a $250 television now buys a suit of clothing instead. Before the tariff he had the freedom to spend $250 on either the suit or the television and chose the television. That choice tells us that he gets more pleasure or usefulness from a television than he does from the suit of clothes when they both have the same price. By placing a tariff on televisions, you eliminate this choice. Instead, you force him to choose between a suit of clothes at $250 and a television for $275. You have forced him to swap the television for a suit of clothes, an exchange that makes him worse off. His loss is the difference in enjoyment between the two."

"I see the point. It is a bit unfair. But only a bit. He does have the suit, after all."

"One man's bit is another man's bitterness, but let's not argue."

"At least you admit, Dave, that the tariff produced more American jobs."

"I beg your pardon."

"I said at least you'll admit that the tariff created American jobs."

"Ed. You're a fine man, an intelligent man. But after all we have been through together, how can you say that a tariff produces jobs?"

"Doesn't it? I hired more workers than I did before, didn't I? Isn't that an increase in jobs?"

"Ed, do you remember the roundabout way to wealth?"

"Sure."

"What is it?"

"Sometimes it's cheaper to produce televisions in the roundabout way than the direct way. There are two ways to prod—"

"All right. Do you see a relationship between what we are talking about now and the roundabout way to wealth?"

"Not really. The roundabout way is a theory about production costs. My increase in workers and their wages isn't some abstract theory. Those changes are real. Those are real cars they're driving. The increase in jobs has to be good for America."

"Really? Let's go back to Rahway, New Jersey."

So we closed our eyes and headed to the northeast again.

"What do you see, Ed?"

"Nothing."

"Do you know where we are?"

"Looks like a corn field."

"It is. This corn field stands where the Merck pharmaceutical company used to stand."

"Where did it go?"

"Nowhere. It was never built in the first place. Remember, we are in the 1995 when there are no imports because all foreign products are banned. Without free trade, this particular plant of Merck's never got built."

"Why, Dave? And what's that have to do with a tariff on televisions?"

"When America makes goods for herself instead of importing them, some American factories expand, giving the impression that jobs are being created. But the people to fill those jobs have to come from somewhere."

"Come on, Dave. Are you telling me that because America stopped importing televisions and expanded domestic production, Merck never built this plant?"

"Yes."

"How can that be?"

"In a sense, there is absolutely no relationship between a television factory expansion and a pharmaceutical plant that is never built. Yet they are intimately related in so many ways. Because you and other American television manufacturers hired workers for your plant, this plant didn't have the workers available to staff it."

"But, Dave. You admitted before that workers in a television plant can't become chemists overnight. So how can chemists turn into television manufacturing workers?"

"Overnight, no. But their children can, don't you see? With free trade, some of the children of your workers became chemists and marketing people working for Merck. Without free trade, making televisions suddenly looks more attractive than studying chemistry. The children of your workers didn't go on to graduate school to study chemistry."

"Why not?"

"Because the wages of chemists were less than they would be under free trade."

"Why?"

"Two reasons. First, as you admitted earlier, when there is an expansion of the television industry, the wages of television workers rise. But the second reason is less obvious. Without imports, the demand for pharmaceuticals, via the roundabout way, is less than it was before. As a result, the wages of chemists are lower than they were before."

"Why is the demand lower? I thought we agreed that at least with a tariff, the higher price of televisions was a wash, some Americans got richer while others got poorer by nearly the same amount. If Americans have roughly the same amount of wealth, why will the demand for pharmaceuticals go down?"

"Think hard and you tell me, Ed."

"OK. If American demand for pharmaceutical products stays the same, does someone else's fall?"

"Whose demand might fall?"

"Japan's."

"Why?"

"Well, that's what I'm having trouble figuring out. Nothing has changed in Japan to change the demand for pharmaceutical products."

"Are you sure?"

"No, I'm not. I bet you are though."

"I admit to having an inkling. Before trade restrictions, America produced some of its televisions in the roundabout way. America produced drugs and swapped them for televisions. With either a tariff or quota on foreign televisions, fewer Japanese televisions come into the United States. But with fewer Japanese televisions coming into the United States, the Japanese have fewer dollars. They, or the nations that trade with Japan to get dollars, will buy less of those things that dollars can buy, such as pharmaceuticals. American exporting industries will suffer."

"I don't know, Dave. It's hard to believe that just because there are fewer American dollars in the hands of Japanese people that they are going to be less interested in buying American pharmaceuticals."

"The money hides the real interactions between Americans and Japanese. Suppose you are a farmer. You grow food. By specializing in food, you get very good at growing it. There's a tailor in town who is good at making clothes. You barter with the tailor, swapping some of the food you grow for the clothes the tailor makes. One night, before going to bed, you take a stupidity potion. You wake up stupid and say, 'I'm not going to let those clothes-making jobs get out of my household. I am going to ban imports of clothing.' So you announce to the tailor in town that you are no longer going to import any clothing. What do you think happens to your sales of food to the tailor?"

"They're going to go down."

"They're not just going to go down. They're going to disappear. Can you see why?"

"If I'm not going to trade my food, he isn't going to give me his clothing out of the goodness of his heart."

"Exactly. Your refusal to import clothes is equivalent to saying you don't want to swap clothes for food. And you're not going to make up food sales by selling more to the carpenter who works on your house. The carpenter isn't any more interested in your food than he was before. The same thing is going on when the United States puts a tariff on televisions. America is saying to the world—we don't want to trade as much as we did before. As a result, the United States is going to make more televisions and less of something else. America makes less of whatever it is Americans used to swap with foreigners for those televisions. Imports and exports are inextricably tied together."

"So the increase in American television workers is offset by a decrease in workers in industries that shipped goods to Japan or to some other foreign nation."

"Exactly. And that is why a tariff does not avoid the short-term hardship caused by foreign competition. A tariff creates its own short-run hardship. It is just harder to observe."

"Is the offset exact? Are the number of television jobs gained exactly the same as the number of export jobs lost?"

"That is really the wrong question. The number of jobs in America is determined by the population and the proportion of the population wanting to work. The real issue isn't the number of jobs, but the kind of jobs people are doing. America should have its citizens work in the areas that allow the best application of their skills. Otherwise there are lost opportunities to create wealth. A tariff creates two kinds of losses for Americans. Because televisions have become more expensive, too few televisions are purchased by Americans. The televisions that are still enjoyed by Americans are produced at an inefficiently high cost. America devotes more resources to producing televisions domestically than are necessary."

"Why, Dave?"

"The Merck pharmaceutical factory which once produced televisions in the roundabout way has been replaced by a Stellar television factory making televisions the direct way. Do you remember how Merck produces a television? They produce drugs sold in Japan. Take one of Merck's pharmaceutical products, one particular drug. Think of the cost to Merck to produce enough doses of the drug equaling the value of a television. Selling that number of doses in Japan is equivalent to producing a television by the roundabout way. The cost of producing that number of doses is lower than your cost of producing a television the direct way. Merck produces a television more efficiently. You could take the resources from your factory, turn them into a pharmaceutical factory, and still have resources left over for America to produce something else of value."

"I saw before that televisions did get a lot cheaper under free trade. Let's go look and see what happened to the price of a television when they are produced the direct way."

I took Ed back to Willie's Appliance Store where we looked at some 1995 televisions under tariffs. They were a lot more expensive than they were at Circuit City under free trade.

"But why, Dave, why? Why are they so expensive?"

"It is that old theory of comparative advantage we talked about before. The roundabout way to wealth. Is the farmer who makes his own shirts richer or poorer? He looks richer because he has kept the shirt industry within his household. But in fact he is poorer. Because he fails to concentrate on making food, he becomes a poorer farmer. Making the shirt is expensive because it means giving up time and skills better spent at farming. That is the America you see around you today with trade restrictions. It is a country that must do everything for itself. There are not enough people and machines and land to go around to make everything as cheaply as could be made under free trade. All the skills that were unleashed in pharmaceuticals and computers and—"

"What about my son Steve?"

"We will go see Steve. But before we do, I want you to think about the factory in Rahway that never was."

"The pharmaceutical plant?"

"Yes. In many ways it is the essence of the matter."

"Strange that something that doesn't exist should be the essence of the matter."

"When imports cause a television factory to lay off workers we understand their pain and suffering and feel sympathy for them. But when a tariff eliminates jobs at a pharmaceutical plant, the relationship is such a roundabout one that no one even notices it when it occurs. No one blames the tariff for the hardship in Rahway, but hardship is there nevertheless. Everyone believes that a tariff prevents the unemployment of the television or automobile workers. They don't see the tariff causing the unemployment of the pharmaceutical workers. The tariff is praised when the television plant is built. No one sees the pharmaceutical plant or computer plant that is never built. It is hard to see something that doesn't exist.

"And here is another irony, Ed. When an American buys an American car, he congratulates himself for helping to provide American jobs. Never mind that half or more of the parts in the car come from overseas or Canada or Mexico. American auto manufacturers have convinced most Americans that buying American is good for American jobs. But do you see the irony? An American who buys a Japanese car is also helping to create American jobs. But not in the car industry. The buyer of the Japanese car stimulates those industries that trade with Japan. The buyer of the Japanese car helps the Boeing worker, the chemist at Procter & Gamble, the Merck worker, the Disney cartoonists, and the workers in those industries that export American know-how around the world. It is not a question of creating jobs, but which jobs to create."

"I see the irony, Dave, but you can see how hard it is for people to see the full effects."

"I do. And that explains much of the politics behind trade protection. When Frank Bates pushes a bill to help the television industry, who favors it?"

"My workers, for one."

"How intense is their support?"

"A lot is at stake for them. They will write Frank letters and go see him when he visits from Washington. Their union will make contributions to Frank and the workers will vote for him next election."

"Who should oppose Frank's bill, Ed?"

"Consumers."

"That's right. But the interest of the consumer is quite weak. The consumer only has $25 or so at stake, not the hundreds of dollars that your workers are fighting for. Naturally, the consumer is less motivated to get involved. Consumers feel guilty getting involved. All they hear over and over again is that it is their patriotic duty to support domestic industry. Tell me, Ed, what do you think is a consumer's patriotic duty?"

"I thought I knew. But I see now that it is more complicated than I once thought. I would hope people would buy my televisions. But if they don't, I guess it doesn't hurt America, it just helps some Americans and hurts others."

"But most consumers don't see that, so they feel guilty buying foreign products or fighting trade protection. Of course there is another group besides consumers who should fight protection."

"Those Merck workers, right?"

"Correct, Ed. Unfortunately, their opposition is muted."

"Why?"

"For one, while it is obvious that television workers stand to gain from a tariff on imported televisions, it is not always obvious which industries are harmed. Even worse, they may not even exist to fight for their self-interest. A law that preserves the television industry but harms the computer industry should be opposed by the workers in the computer industry, for example, who will not have the opportunities they would have had. But they may not be working in the industry yet. Take Steven, your son—"

"Can we go see him, Dave?"

"We will see him, Ed, I promise. Soon. But think of the Steven of 35 years ago, the Steven of 1960. In 1960, Steven is a child. He doesn't see how the protection of the television industry hurts the companies that trade with the rest of the world. He can't see how protection brings resources into the television industry and prevents other domestic industries such as computers from expanding. How can you expect him, child or adult, to oppose a law whose effects will not be felt for thirty years? But someone should be looking out for the children to make sure they have the opportunity to pursue their wildest dreams. Don't you think so, Ed?"

CHAPTER EIGHT

Tariffs vs. Quotas

"That's all well and good, Dave. But Frank Bates's original bill was a quota, not a tariff. They seem pretty different to me."

"There is a difference, but I doubt we're thinking along the same lines. What do you think the difference is?"

"A tariff is like a tax on foreigners. But a quota just reduces the amount of foreign supply that can come in. A quota gets the American consumer to substitute an American-made product for the foreign one."

"Ed, what do you think happens when there are fewer foreign televisions available?"

"Foreign televisions get more expensive, I'd guess."

"And with fewer foreign televisions available at a higher price, what do you think happens to the demand for American televisions?"

"Goes up. And so will the price, won't it, Dave? Hmm. It does sound something like a tariff."

"In fact, the same chain of events occurs. In response to the higher price for their product, domestic television producers expand their production. Both American and foreign-made televisions end up being more expensive. With an increase in price, consumers are harmed. Americans have fewer televisions to enjoy than they did before, and too many televisions are made domestically using the direct way and too few made the roundabout way."

"I'm still confused about why the total number of televisions has to go down. Why can't the expansion of American production make up for the lost foreign imports caused by the quota?"

"Here is why. With a quota, there is a reduction in foreign supply causing an increase in the price of televisions. In response to the increase in price, American production expands. But it can never equal or outweigh the reduction in foreign supply. Suppose it matched the decrease in foreign supply. Then the total combined supply of domestic and foreign televisions to U.S. consumers would be back to where it was before. But if production is back to what it was before, then price will be the same as it was

54

before the quota. But then you would have a contradiction. Why would American manufacturers like yourself have expanded production if the price ends up unchanged? And if you do so by mistake, you will close some plants when you see that the new price is equal to the old one. Not all of those new plants can be profitable at the old price or you would have opened them before. The net effect of a quota is a decrease in supply and a higher price of televisions both domestic and imported."

"It does sound a lot like a tariff."

"In fact, you can structure a quota to mimic a tariff perfectly. Suppose America imports 20 million televisions in the absence of tariffs and quotas. Suppose that when you put a tariff of $25 in place, price goes from $250 to $275 and imports fall by 25% to 15 million televisions. You can have the exact same effect on the price of televisions by limiting the number of foreign televisions to 15 million. Price will go up to $275 just as it did under the tariff."

"Is there any difference between a tariff and a quota in those two situations, Dave?"

"A quota of 15 million mimics almost all of the effects of a $25 tariff in the example I described. In both cases, televisions in the stores will sell for $275. The difference is that in the case of a tariff, part of that higher price is captured by the American government in the form of tariff revenue."

"How does that work?"

"With a $25 tariff, the importer of the televisions has to pay the government $25. So while the consumer loses $25 on the imported televisions, at least some American will be the beneficiary of the $25 worth of government revenue when it is spent. Remember that from the standpoint of looking at all Americans, the gains and losses from the $25 by itself cancel out."

"Why do you say 'by itself'?"

"Because the money changing hands from the consumer to the government to the beneficiary of government spending is a wash. One American, the consumer, is $25 poorer, while another American, the beneficiary of government spending, is $25 richer. Whether that transfer from one American to another is fair is a separate question. But what is not a wash is the effect of that $25 transfer on people's behavior. Fewer televisions get enjoyed and America devotes too many resources to producing televisions directly instead of through the roundabout way. That is not a wash. That is a net loss that makes America poorer."

"How does the quota differ?"

"In the case of the quota, you still get the losses from too few televisions purchased and too many resources going to produce televisions directly. But the extra $25 paid by the consumer for the foreign-made televisions goes either to the American importer who brings in the televisions from abroad or to the foreign producer. If it is the latter, the foreign producer has $25 more American dollars to buy up pharmaceuticals and computers and other American products."

"What's wrong with that?"

"With a tariff, that $25 of purchasing power and claims on American goods and services stays in American hands. With a quota, that $25 may end up in the hands of foreign producers. This allows foreigners to lay claim to American goods and services, leaving fewer computers, drugs, and other goods for Americans to enjoy. A tariff makes sure that those goods stay in American hands."

"But you told me before that when foreigners have dollars they stimulate the American companies that export, such as Merck and Boeing."

"They do, but it would be better for America if foreigners kept the dollars and never 'stimulated' our economy. America would much rather have free televisions than have to swap drugs and airplanes for them. Then Americans would be able to enjoy more drugs and airplanes instead of the Japanese. But Japan isn't interested in giving away televisions. They expect something in return. In the case we are discussing, the question is who will have $25 to spend, Americans or foreigners? It is always better for America if Americans have the extra $25 instead of the foreigners. That way the extra $25 worth of goods stays in America instead of going to Japan."

"What determines whether Americans running import businesses or foreign suppliers get to keep the extra $25?"

"It depends on how the quota is structured. Under a standard quota, the government hands out licenses to importers giving them the right to import a particular amount of the good being restricted. Under this system, the importers lucky enough to get the licenses enjoy the extra $25, in the form of higher prices."

"What determines which importers are the lucky ones?"

"Ah. In fact, luck has little to do with it. Under a tariff, the government has an extra $25 for every imported television to spend on government programs. Under a quota the government also has $25 after a fashion, in the form of licenses it can distribute to importers. As you might expect, this is not done randomly."

"I assume importers compete in currying favor with government officials to be the beneficiaries of government largesse."

"I assume so as well. Such competition wastes resources from the perspective of the economy as a whole and is an extra cost of a quota. Sometimes the government will give out the licenses to those who have been importers in the past. But even this seemingly innocent choice is likely to be subject to pressure of various kinds."

"How can a quota lead to foreign suppliers capturing the $25 increase in the price of televisions, Dave?"

"This occurs when the government institutes a 'voluntary' quota."

"What's a voluntary quota?"

"A voluntary quota is when a foreign nation agrees 'voluntarily' to restrict its exports to a fixed number. These quotas are sometimes called VERs for 'Voluntary Export Restraints' or VRAs for 'Voluntary Restraint Agreements.' The only thing voluntary about such quotas is the name. An ugly extortionary element comes into play. The United States government tells the Japanese government: 'We would like you to restrict the number of Japanese cars coming into the United States to such-and-such.' "

"And if they say no?"

"If they say no, the government can impose a 'real' quota."

"What is the advantage of having the quota seem voluntary?"

"One advantage is that no American politician has to go on record officially supporting a quota. The other advantage is that in principle it is more flexible. In theory, the American government could ask the Japanese to relax or contract the quota without having to go to Congress. In practice they are much like a legislated quota. But there is a difference in who captures the profits from higher prices. With a standard, or 'involuntary' quota, U.S. importers control the scarce licenses and make higher profits from the higher prices paid by consumers. With a voluntary quota, the foreign government determines who gets to export the goods to America. The foreign government is given the scarce and valuable rights rather than American importers. As importers compete to get at the scarce supply of foreign goods, the price again gets driven up an additional $25. But now foreigners capture the money."

"Did America ever use voluntary quotas to limit imports, Dave?"

"Not if Frank Bates gets elected in 1960. A Frank Bates election leads to an America of complete self-sufficiency—no imports. That is the world we are in now where Star looks like it used to and everyone drives a Ford Fairlane or Chevy Impala. In this world, quotas have no meaning because there is nothing to limit."

"But what about the America where Frank Bates is not elected?"

"Then America follows a path of increasingly free trade. That was the world we saw earlier tonight. But even in such a world, American producers were sometimes able to reduce foreign competition using tariffs, quotas, and other means. For example, in 1981, the United States asked the Japanese to limit their exports of cars 'voluntarily.' As you would expect, these limits increased the price of both domestic and imported cars to the American consumer. Economists estimated the effect on the price of an American car from the 'voluntary' restriction of Japanese imports to be at least $400 per car. In 1984, for example, that meant that consumers paid an extra $4 billion dollars to American auto makers and their workers because of the restriction on imports. But quotas, voluntary or legislated, had wider effects still."

"For example?"

"Many Japanese auto manufacturers built factories in the United

States to get around the limit. This appeared to save American jobs, but it only saved American jobs in the auto industry. If the voluntary quota had been removed and more foreign cars imported, there would have been an expansion of jobs in those markets producing goods for the Japanese. Moreover, this would have allowed Americans to specialize in some activities with the benefits from specialization—increased innovation and performance from increased familiarity with the tasks. The roundabout way to wealth we spoke of long ago. In addition, there were inefficiencies resulting from the Japanese building a plant in America that might have been better placed in Japan."

"But might not the Japanese want to put a factory in America, anyway, to be closer to American customers? They could save transportation costs and gain knowledge of the consumer more easily."

"If such a move made economic sense, they would do so without the quota. Japanese car companies started building car factories in the United States beginning in 1982, the year after the 'voluntary' quota went into effect. Between 1982 and 1990, six Japanese car companies built factories. But cars were just one example of 'voluntary' quotas."

"What was another?"

"There were many. The case of televisions will interest you. Remember when I told you that your American competitors had stopped making televisions?"

"Yes."

"Here is what happened. Zenith saw its profits fall because of foreign competition. This kind of pressure is the reverse of a tariff. As prices charged by foreign competitors fall, American suppliers are forced to lower price in order to compete. Zenith charged foreign producers with dumping and asked the government to punish their competitors."

"Did they win?"

"They did not, despite the government's flexible definition of what constitutes dumping. But they did get some legislative relief while the case was in progress. The government imposed an 'Orderly Marketing Arrangement.' "

"That's a mouthful."

"It's just a fancy and uninformative name for a voluntary quota. It restricted imports of foreign televisions."

"Did it help?"

"It induced the foreign manufacturers to build assembly plants in the United States to get around the law, as had happened in the automobile industry. That was part of the reason why you were able to sell your company to the Japanese in the world of free trade we visited earlier, and why they kept the plant outside of Chicago open as an assembly plant. Even when the 'Arrangement' expired, foreign manufacturers continued to build plants here in fear of future 'Arrangements.' Here is the irony. While foreign companies were moving plants to America, Zenith was moving the bulk of its production to Mexico."

"It does sound a bit cockeyed."

"Rather unattractive, wasn't it, Ed? By getting the government to impose a voluntary quota, Zenith forced its competitors to go to the expense of building plants in the United States and using more expensive American workers. Meanwhile they did much of their production in low-wage Mexico."

"But it didn't work?"

"It did not. Once Zenith lost the dumping case, they were through. The court's decision was applauded by believers in free trade and lampooned as naive by the protectionists. But those protectionists could never explain why the prices of televisions remained low, relative to wages, as we saw when we visited Circuit City."

"What else happens because of quotas, Dave?"

"With the 'voluntary' quotas of the 1980s, because the quota was expressed in a fixed number of cars, the Japanese manufacturers sent over cars loaded with features. Normally, in an unregulated market, they would send over a mix of cars, some with many features such as air-conditioning and so on, while other cars would be a basic model sold at a lower price. Because they could only send over a fixed number, the Japanese sent over the fanciest, most expensive models. Consumers had fewer choices."

"How did the Japanese government decide which manufacturers got to send their cars to fill the limit."

"That is another source of inefficiency. I presume that the Japanese manufacturers competed to curry favor with their government in order to receive the precious slots in the American market. Just as U.S. importers compete to get licenses from the U.S. government under a standard quota, the resources used to persuade the Japanese government served no productive purpose. Initiative and energy that normally would have served the consumer got sidetracked because of the quota. A similar phenomenon occurred in America as American auto dealers made profits from the scarce foreign cars they were selling. Every car produced a large profit, but cars were scarce. How could a dealer insure a steady supply of cars? The supply could not be steady because the quota fixed the supply. Dealers bribed and cajoled the manufacturer's representatives to get increased access to the limited number of cars. Again, this energy was diverted from serving the consumer."

"I see your point, Dave. I just wonder about how important it is."

"Energy and initiative, like all commodities, are not in infinite supply. In a world of free trade, American producers are forced to keep up and surpass foreign ingenuity. In a world of restricted trade, producers spend their time trying to lobby the government for ever-wider restrictions."

"So Frank Bates's complete ban on foreign imports ends that problem."

"Yes, it does. It also ends the spur of foreign competition. Remember that first trip you made to Washington to see Frank Bates about protection for the television industry? That trip took time and energy. Instead of looking for a better way to make televisions, you lobbied Frank Bates to keep out your competitors. And when you got your way, and Frank Bates passed the bill protecting you and your industry, did the loss of foreign competition change the amount of time you put in trying to improve your product? Tell me, Ed. How did you know that those cars people were driving in the America without imports were Ford Fairlanes?"

"Come on, Dave. I know what a Ford Fairlane looks like."

"Yes, and it looks the same in 1995 as it did in 1960. Wonder why?"

"OK, I get your point. There is less competition. But isn't there a benefit from fewer model changes? You save on design costs and retooling."

"Perhaps. Consumers like variety. For those that don't, some companies keep their models unchanged for many years. But such savings or losses from less variety are of secondary importance compared to the more important effects. The key change is that without foreign competition, American car manufacturers got lazy and less innovative. The Ford Fairlane is a perfect example."

"But, Dave, it's a pretty good car."

"Yes, it is. But we didn't have a chance to look closely at the cars in 1995 when there was free trade. Remember that Honda Accord you were leaning on, back in the parking lot of the movie theater? It had air bags, anti-lock brakes, and an FM radio that could play pre-recorded tapes. Compared to the Fairlane, it was structurally safer in a crash even if the air bags and anti-lock brakes malfunctioned. It could travel 50% farther on a tank of gas. It didn't burn oil and broke down much less often."

"What are air bags and anti-lock brakes?"

"Safety features that will never be on that Ford Fairlane. When Ford finally designed a car that could compete with the Honda, called the Taurus, it had all those features of the Accord and then some. Do you think Ford would have made the Taurus if the Honda Accord was kept in Japan?"

---------------- CHAPTER NINE ----------------

Road Trip

I could see that Ed was getting a bit fatigued by his immersion in economics, so I decided to give him a break. A major road trip was in order. We had visited the New Jersey of 1995 twice already, but I had a more scenic and traditional trip planned for Ed, with an ulterior educational motive.

Ed, growing up in Star, hadn't been to the big cities of America too often. So I invited him to take advantage of my powers and tour the tourist attractions of America in the year 1995 when America is free of imports. As we walked together, we only saw American cars on the streets, as it had been in Star. We visited New York, Chicago, Boston, and San Francisco. We saw the Statue of Liberty, the Miracle Mile, the Freedom Trail, and the Golden Gate Bridge. Then we headed down to Washington, D.C., for the standard tourist attractions: the Washington Monument, the Lincoln Memorial, the Jefferson Memorial. Ed enjoyed himself immensely.

We sat on the Mall in Washington, the Washington Monument looming ahead, Congress behind.

"This is a great country, Dave, even without foreign goods. It makes me so proud."

"It is not my country, but I too admire America. Tell me, Ed. Did you notice anything unusual about the places we've visited?"

"Not really. I haven't had a chance to visit the tourist attractions of Washington since I was a kid. Too busy making televisions, I guess. They don't seem to have changed as far as I can tell."

"Notice anything unusual about the visitors?"

"Not really. A lot of school kids as you would expect to see in Washington. Nothing else really grabbed my attention."

"Did you hear any foreign accents while we waited in line?"

"No."

"Did you see any Japanese taking pictures?"

"No."

"Notice any foreign tourists at all?"

"I guess I didn't. Is that unusual?"

"Oh, yes. In the old days, before imports were eliminated, Washington teemed with people from all over the world. The streets of New York would be filled with foreign tourists, rich and poor. And San Francisco, one of the world's most beautiful cities, would always attract visitors from abroad. But no longer."

"Why not?"

"How does a foreign tourist pay a hotel bill or a restaurant meal?"

"I don't know. Traveler's checks, cash."

"But, Ed, they have to be in dollars. How would a citizen of Tokyo get dollars? Or a Frenchman? Or an Englishman? Or a West German?"

"He would go to his bank and—"

"But where would his bank get dollars, Ed? A bank only has dollars if there are some Americans willing to swap dollars for francs or yen or pounds. If no foreign goods are allowed into the country, then Americans are not spending dollars on exports. With no money spent on exports, foreign banks have no dollars to swap for the domestic currencies of their own country."

"I never thought of tourism that way."

"The purchases of a tourist in America are really the same as exports. When a foreign tourist spends a night in a New York hotel, it is the same as shipping goods abroad without paying a transportation fee. It is the same with a restaurant meal. A restaurant meal eaten by a foreign tourist is the same as shipping food abroad. A foreign tourist's expenditures are a way to export goods and services in a funny way. Instead of shipping the food there, the foreigner comes and picks the food up here. The tourist pays the freight charge."

"The concept of exporting services is a strange one."

"Yes, but potentially very important. An extraordinary example of such an export is university education. America has the best universities in the world and under free trade foreign students can come to America to enjoy that service. Without trade, those students don't have the dollars to spend on American education. At Washington University, where your daughter Susan earned her MBA, when there is free trade about 25% of the students come from overseas. In fact, Susan was the president of a student club promoting activities for international business. She brought speakers in from Japan and even spent the summer between her first and second year of classes in a summer internship in Hong Kong."

"Susan spent a summer in Hong Kong as a student?"

"She did in the world of free trade. Without free trade, well—"

"Well?"

"Be patient. We'll see Susan soon. The point is that foreign students enriched Susan's view of the world and opened her eyes beyond the midwest until she could see beyond the Pacific. That's why she ended up working for Mast Industries and The Limited under free trade. You can imagine how studying together with foreign students makes the world a cozier place. And how tourists to and from America build ties between nations."

"Are there no tourists visiting America? Are no Americans visiting foreign countries?"

"There are a few. Americans who can afford to travel supply a handful of dollars while they are abroad that form a pool of American money for tourists who wish to visit here. But the government eventually had to limit the number of foreign visitors and immigrants as well, even if they could have acquired dollars."

"Why would the government do that?"

"Smuggling. When you ban foreign imports, quality declines and price increases. Goods get more expensive. This creates a black market in imports. Foreigners would come to America pretending to be tourists. Their real goal was to swap their cheaper foreign goods to Americans for dollars to pay for American goods."

"Come on, Dave. How much stuff could people bring in as tourists?"

"A lot more than you can imagine. A lot of goods came over the Mexican and Canadian borders. Boats landed at night all along the American coastline. People would smuggle the goods in, and use the dollars to buy American goods or to enjoy American life for a while as a tourist. You have to remember the profits available. Don't you think it would be worthwhile to try and smuggle coffee into America? Or shirts by wearing a few extra? Or diamonds? The government had to put a lot of people to work stopping the smuggling. To save costs they put a lot of restrictions on legal entry into the United States. So there aren't a lot of tourists. And not many Americans have any foreign currency to take abroad. So Americans take a lot of trips to Washington D.C. and other American cities."

"It's sad."

"Yes, it is. A lot of hotels and restaurants went out of business."

"And there is a lot less communication between people. That can't be healthy."

"No, I don't think so either. You're lucky I made it through customs. Special visa."

We sat in silence and looked out over the panorama of monuments that make up the Washington skyline. I had an idea.

"Ed, let's make one more stop before we get back to business."

"Sure. Where to?"

"Close your eyes. Now open them."

"We're in England, Dave! There's a real English pub! I've always dreamed of having a beer in an English pub. Is there some way we can have a drink in there despite our unreal existence?"

"Go and see. Ask for yourself."

"Money is going to be a bit of a problem. I've only got a few American coins. But, Dave, it would make sense for you to have a few pounds on you. Can we do it?"

"I'm afraid finance is not my line anymore. But we shall see what develops. Belly up to the bar, as the expression goes. See what happens."

We headed inside.

"The place is deserted, Dave. There's no one here. The taps are dry."

"I'm sorry to disappoint you, Ed."

"This place gives me the creeps. Are we in some London slum?"

"Let's go outside and look around. Perhaps we can get our bearings."

We wandered back out into bright sunlight. We were on a winding cobblestoned street, then suddenly a clearing.

"Where have you brought me, Dave? What's that funny structure across the lagoon there?"

"That is a bit of the Eiffel Tower."

"But that's in France, Dave. And what are those other strange buildings? They're all falling down. Is that a pagoda?"

"This is what was known as Epcot Center, Ed. Built by the Walt Disney Company, it was an incredible tourist attraction. Tourists came from all over the world and America to enjoy it. This part was called the World Showcase. Nations of the world built pavilions to capture the flavor of their countries. There were movies on screens that surrounded you, extraordinary displays of a nation's heritage, art, and food and drink. When America stopped trading with the rest of the world, the foreign tourists stopped coming. At first, Epcot had a bit of a renaissance. Americans couldn't go abroad so they came here to satisfy their thirst for things foreign. But Disney eventually lost so much money, they shut it down. No one cares about it anymore. It's falling apart."

"It makes my skin crawl."

"You should have been here when the sun sparkled on the lake. In front of the Japanese pavilion, a Japanese artist blew what looked like glass into the shapes of animals and fish. As each delicate piece was completed, he would give them to the mesmerized children gathered around him. Only it was not glass but spun sugar. What a delicious dilemma for a child. There was street theater here in these English streets, and, yes, the warm English beer flowed. I tell you—"

"Please stop, Dave. Take us back to Star."

"As you wish."

CHAPTER TEN

The Case for Protection

"You make it out to be so black and white, Dave. Maybe tariffs and quotas don't produce jobs. But there are other reasons for protecting some industries from foreign competition."

"For example?"

"National security. America doesn't want to be dependent on foreigners for anything with military significance. They could blackmail us."

"What type of product is vital in times of war?"

"Steel."

"Steel is not as essential as it once was. Titanium is more critical. But let's consider steel because America's steel producers never seem to tire of asking for protection. But even if America's security depended on steel, keeping out cheap foreign steel isn't necessary if steel comes from many different nations and some of them are allies. It is hard to imagine that all steel producers will be America's enemies in time of war. Even so, what size steel industry do you think is necessary to be a springboard for wartime production? In World War II America was able to increase its steel production enormously under wartime mobilization. I think America could do it again very quickly. In the meanwhile, America would have the enormous stock of planes and tanks she has already amassed."

"Dave, are you admitting that a tariff on steel might be justifiable if our steel came from enemies we might fight in a war?"

"Sure, in theory, under that unlikely condition. In practice, it might be wiser to create either a public or private strategic reserve to avoid the threat of blackmail. But you can be sure that businessmen in many industries will do all they can to convince people that their product is vital for national security."

"What about a case for protection when an industry is just starting out? Without protection it will be destroyed by foreign competition. When the industry matures, tariffs or quotas can be removed."

"Ah, the infant industry argument. Virtually all businesses and industries lose money at the start. That is what an investment is all about.

You give up money today for a greater sum tomorrow. Either the money you make later is enough to compensate for the amount you lose at the start, or it is not. If it is great enough, then you do not need protection. If the money you make later does not make up for the initial losses, then protection is a mistake. You are protecting an investment that never should have been made in the first place."

"But what if foreign competitors lower their prices to make those initial losses unbearable? Without the help of a tariff to make things fair, how are they going to get started?"

"Ed, it is similar to the discussion we had about Japanese rice. It is a theoretical possibility that foreign competitors would squash an American upstart. Even this possibility requires foreign competitors to be willing to sustain the massive losses necessary to absorb all of the demand for their product that low prices produce. If they do not, the American competitor will be able to sell their output at a higher price. Where is the evidence that it has ever occurred? When did an American industry begin production only to give up in the face of cutthroat pricing by foreign competitors? Followed by an increase in price by those foreign competitors. For this argument to be sustained empirically, you have to make a completely untestable, unverifiable claim."

"Yes, Dave?"

"You have to claim that the threat of foreign competition is so insidious, so conspiratorial, so effective, that American companies never came into existence in the first place. I find this argument uncompelling."

"So much for the infant industry argument. Are there any other arguments in favor of protection?"

"There is no end to the creativity of business in finding arguments for government assistance. As Milton Friedman has pointed out, every businessman favors free markets while arguing that his own industry has special circumstances justifying government intervention in the national interest. But even academic economists sometimes make at least a theoretical case in favor of protection."

"Let's hear one."

"Consider a large country such as the United States, whose demand for a product makes up a substantial part of the world market."

"Say for televisions."

"Correct, at least at certain times. The argument for protection goes like this. If America is a large demander of televisions, then a tariff that reduces the demand for televisions by the Americans can actually reduce the price of televisions."

"A tax reduces the price?"

"Not the full price to the consumer including the tariff. That still rises. But the price of the television before the tariff is added on can actually go down. Suppose again that televisions are selling initially for $250. A

$25 tariff will typically increase the price to $275. This assumes that the prices of televisions in other parts of the world are unaffected and stay at $250. Because they stay at $250 everywhere else in the world, the price in America must go to $275 when the tariff of $25 is put on. Otherwise foreign sellers would not be willing to bring a television into America."

"Makes sense."

"But price will not jump the full amount of the tariff if the United States has a sufficiently large share of the world television market. In this case, when America puts a tariff in place, American sales still go down. But this reduction is a significant reduction in world-wide sales, because we are assuming the United States is a large part of the world market. Foreign producers will try to sell the televisions they used to sell in America else-where. In the case where the United States is a small part of the world mar-ket, it is easy to sell those televisions somewhere else without lowering price. But if the lost sales in the United States are a large part of the world market, they will have to lower their price in order to sell the same number of televisions they did before. Televisions around the world become less expensive. The overall decrease in the world demand for televisions caused by the reduction in the size of the American market could lower the price of televisions to say $240. When you add in the $25 tariff, the price only goes to $265 instead of $275."

"But aren't consumers still going to be worse off?"

"Yes. Consumers will be worse off by $15. But America will have revenue from the tariff from each television of $25. So there is a net gain to the United States of $10 per television. Essentially, the United States has acted like a cartel of customers rather than the typical case where there is a cartel of sellers. A cartel of sellers withholds supply to get a higher price. In this case, the United States withholds demand to get a lower price."

"Sounds pretty good."

"Its attractiveness is what motivated a great economist, Edgeworth, to say that this argument in favor of tariffs should be put in the medicine chest but labeled 'Poison.' "

"Why, Dave?"

"While theoretically beneficial, in practice there is no guarantee that the benefits will come to pass."

"Why not?"

"Many reasons. You may think you can affect the world price of televisions, when in fact, your impact is negligible. Most countries, even the United States, make a trivial contribution to the world demand for any product."

"But if demand is reduced from one country, isn't the price around the world going to fall at least a small amount?"

"Probably not. Suppose you think the price of apples is too high and you stop eating apples. What happens to the price of apples in the super-market?"

"Nothing."

"Exactly. And the reason is that in the world market for apples, taking out your demand has an insignificant effect on the world apple market. Now suppose every citizen of the state of Illinois stopped eating apples. What is the effect on the price of apples?"

"I give up."

"The answer again is nothing. The citizens of Illinois make up such a small part of the apple market that removing their demand has a negligible effect on price."

"But, Dave. If Americans stopped eating apples, wouldn't the price go down?"

"Probably. But I will give you an example to suggest otherwise. Do you know that the American government borrows money to help finance government activity?"

"Sure, and it makes me plenty nervous. Our national debt is way too big."

"I've got news for you, Ed. It's going to get a lot bigger. In fact there are years after 1960 when the American government borrows over $400 billion dollars."

"That'll plunge the country into a depression!"

"Why, Ed?"

"Because to get people to buy the bonds, interest rates will go sky high and no private investment will take place."

"That's what people said. Yet interest rates were quite low when U.S. government borrowing was high."

"How could that be?"

"Because even though $400 billion seems like a lot of money, it is not so large when seen in the context of the world market for borrowing. The United States borrowed that money and interest rates hardly moved at all. For the same reason, a tariff on televisions coming into America that lowers American demand for televisions and thus world demand may leave the price around the world unchanged at $250."

"But in the case where America's demand is large enough to affect the world demand for a product, then a tariff is good for the United States?"

"Not so fast. Even in that case you must have great confidence in the government. The government has to be good at two things. First, it has to be good at estimating the effect of the tariff on the world price. What if they pick a tariff that is too large? A large tariff raises price dramatically to the U.S. consumer, causing a large reduction in U.S. and, consequently, world demand. The price of televisions will fall and the government will have the tariff revenue. But consumers are paying higher prices and enjoying fewer televisions. They are harmed. If you make the tariff too big, that harm can outweigh the gains to other Americans from the tariff revenue."

"That should be easy to prevent. Just make sure that the tariff is not too big."

"That sounds easy. But even if you pick a 'small' tariff, if the effect of the tariff on demand in the United States is sufficiently large, you can have an equally disastrous effect."

"So just make sure that you anticipate the effect of the tariff."

"That is not so easy to do. But to make matters worse, guess who has an incentive to make sure the tariff is set at a high level?"

"The domestic producer of televisions, someone like myself?"

"Exactly. The domestic producer argues that his product, say televisions, is a very large share of the world market. He will argue that it is important for the United States to set a large tariff and take advantage of this opportunity to generate revenue from foreigners."

"OK, so watch out for lobbyists."

"Alas, that is not the only problem."

"What else?"

"You have to make sure that the government spends the $25 it has collected from each television wisely. Otherwise the net gain to the United States disappears."

"But if the United States is a large enough demander of the product, and if the tariff is set at the right level, and if the government spends the money wisely, then a tariff can have a beneficial effect?"

"Yes. Except for one small detail."

"I have a suspicion that you are being sarcastic about the size of the detail, Dave."

"I apologize. You are correct. It is no small detail. All of the preceding argument assumes that the rest of the world does nothing when the United States puts a tariff on their goods. There is nothing to stop a foreign producer from retaliating with tariffs on American goods. Even if the initial tariff in America is set carefully, the retaliation can leave America worse off than before."

"So even though there is an argument in favor of a tariff when a country's demand for a product is a significant portion of world demand, you are saying that it can backfire. Are there any other arguments by academics for protection?"

"At least two more. The first argues that being first into a market can be decisive. It is a variant on the infant industry argument."

"It *is* important to be the first into a market."

"Sometimes. Sometimes it is better to be second. Or more accurately, sometimes it is no handicap not to be the first. But it is conceivable that for certain industries or products it is good to be first."

"What does that have to do with protection?"

"Suppose two countries have companies vying to be the first to bring a technology to market. Then you could argue that the government should subsidize its own domestic firm, and punish the foreign firm with protection. That way, the domestic firm gets a large market share early in the battle. In particular, the argument is made that since high technology products lead to many other products, then America should make sure to maintain her edge in high technology products lest other nations come to dominate those markets and enjoy the products that flow from the technology. This will be particularly true for high technology products that may have room in the world market for only one supplier."

"Sounds pretty reasonable. Is this a legitimate argument for a government role in international competition?"

"Perhaps."

"But?"

"There are many questions to be asked. How do you know whether a high technology product will have many 'spin-offs,' as they are called? How do you know when there will be room for only one supplier? Can you think of many examples? Are you sure that being first is such an advantage? Might it not be better to see how the product fares? And, finally, when government is handing out money and favors, why would you be sure that government will choose the right products to protect? Political influence may play a larger role than the overall well-being of the people."

"OK. Are there answers to those questions?"

"Based on economic theory, no, so I would again encourage empirical observation. For example, in the late 1970s the French and British governments teamed up to produce an enormous technological breakthrough called the supersonic transport, or SST. This was a plane designed to fly from New York to London at a speed you will have difficulty comprehending."

"I can't say I've ever flown to London."

"At the time the plane was under design, the standard jet made the trip in about seven hours. The fruit of the SST project was a plane called the Concorde. The Concorde could make the trip in three and a half hours."

"That sounds pretty fabulous, Dave. Think of the savings in time and productivity for the businessmen trying to do business in both London and New York. The Concorde sounds like a case where government sponsored technology paid off."

"In one sense it is a textbook case of the sort of market we are describing. The market for people who wish to travel from New York to London in three and a half hours is a relatively small one. The Concorde, perhaps by being first, has the market all to itself."

"A monopoly?"

"In a sense. There is competition from the flights taking the full seven hours. But if you want to get to London or New York quickly, you must fly the Concorde, or know a dead British economist on a mission to save his soul."

"So how about it, Dave. Is the Concorde a winner?"

"Only for the people who travel on it. For the investors, the British and French taxpayers, it has been an unmitigated disaster."

"But they have a monopoly on the market."

"Yes. But the market is too small at the prices the Concorde must charge to cover its costs. Yes, the Concorde has a monopoly. Yes, the British and the French implemented the technology before anyone else. Unfortunately, it was a very bad investment. Being first has its rewards. But they must be sufficiently large to outweigh the costs or your investment is a poor one."

"How bad an investment was it?"

"The plane was conceived in 1962 but didn't fly until 1976. The investment by 1976 was $4.3 billion. By 1983, revenues covered operating costs, but given the losses in the preceding years, there is no way the investment paid off. They would have been better off putting their money in a savings account."

"I see your point. But it's just one example."

"Let me give you another. But first, note a deeper flaw in the Concorde. The money from the Concorde came from the taxpayers of Britain and France. They implicitly made the investment and came out on the short end. What do you think is the profile of the typical taxpayer in those countries?"

"I don't know."

"Nor do I. But the typical taxpayer is somewhere in the middle-class. Who do you think is the typical traveler on the Concorde?"

"Not a middle-class French or British taxpayer."

"Bravo, Ed. The fare from New York to London and back on the Concorde in 1993 was over $7,000, as much as seven times the cost on slower planes. Only the wealthiest of the wealthy find their time sufficiently valuable or the novelty of the Concorde sufficiently high to pay the premium. Yet the fare does not cover the cost of the trip. The correct price should include the research costs as well as the operating costs. The average taxpayer is subsidizing the wealthy traveler."

"They could fix that, couldn't they, Dave?"

"How?"

"By putting a tax on the traveler. And using the revenue to help the taxpayer."

"Another roundabout idea from our conversation. Interesting. Of course, a price accomplishes exactly the same thing in a private enterprise."

"How is that?"

"Why didn't private companies invest in the Concorde technology on their own? Why did it take the government's subsidies to make the investment profitable? Without the government subsidies, the project was not profitable. And what does it mean to say that a project is not profitable? It means that the price one expects to be able to charge is not high enough to cover the costs of the project. When the price is high enough to cover the costs, the users of the good pay for the benefits they enjoy, not some third party who is forced to contribute."

"But if the costs could not be covered by the price, why did the British and French government enter into the project?"

"The cynical explanation is that the governments paid more attention to the demands of their aerospace companies than to the costs and benefits accruing to the nation as a whole. The more charitable explanation is that either their estimate of the costs and expected fares differed from the estimates of private companies, or the governments hoped for the national advantage which technology supposedly yields."

"Why would they estimate the costs and expected price so poorly?"

"What is their incentive to do so accurately? They have no stock-holders to face, only taxpayers. Taxpayers tend to have fewer places to turn than investors in a private company."

"Did any of those technological benefits come to pass?"

"Not that the eye can see. In fact, as should be clear to you now, the net effect of this project was to make the people of Britain and France poorer. Some individuals benefited as is always the case in these examples. But the net effect on the citizenry was negative."

"I assume you have another story, Dave."

"I do, and it is one close to home. It is called high-definition television."

"What's that?"

"A better television set and signal, one with crisper, better pictures."

"Our sets were always improving, too."

"I know, Ed, but this is an enormous improvement, not a modest one. It's one you didn't see in our trip to Willie's Appliance Store when we looked at the price of American televisions when there is no foreign competition. It is a whole new technology that only gets developed in a world where America avoids the path of Frank Bates and complete protection."

"I'll be honest with you, Dave. I think televisions are pretty important. But it is hard for me to understand why even a dramatic improvement in television quality is an important economic issue."

"I understand. Yet people made an argument for the importance of high-definition television precisely along the lines we are discussing. They argued that high-definition television was important not because it was crucial to the happiness of mankind, but because in the development of such a lucrative new product, other products would be developed that would lead to other breakthroughs."

"What happened?"

"The Japanese began their research long ago, in 1968, through a government-owned broadcasting company called NHK. Twenty-three years later they had their first broadcast of the new technology. The picture was superb. Unfortunately, the television set necessary to receive the picture cost over $8,000."

"Ouch! Not likely to be a big seller."

"Hardly. While the Japanese were developing their technology, so were the Europeans and Americans. The Europeans went roughly the same route as the Japanese using heavy government involvement to keep their hand in the market."

"And what did the American firms do?"

"First they put their hand out, just as you would expect. They asked the government for subsidies just as their counterparts in Europe and Japan did. Otherwise, they argued, the competition wouldn't be fair."

"And?"

"And the government turned them down. In 1989 a request for $1.35 billion dollars was rejected."

"Billion?"

"Oh, yes. Billion. The Japanese and Europeans spent similar amounts. But the Americans were turned down. The government did make a contribution, however. They agreed to referee a contest, a horse race of sorts. The best technology would be adopted by the Federal Communication Commission as the American standard. Those companies going with the best technology would profit, those who backed the wrong research route would be out of luck."

"What happened?"

"The American companies chose to pursue a completely different technology from that chosen by the Japanese and the Europeans. It turned out to be the better system, despite the late start. Or perhaps because of it. Here is a case where late entry into a market may have been an advantage. The Americans chose a technology with the benefit of having seen what the Japanese and the Europeans did."

"You're saying, Dave, that even though this was an infant industry, and even though it was a chance to dominate the market, the American companies did well without government protection or subsidy. It's an interesting story and impressive. But it's only one story. You can't generalize on the basis of one story."

"I quite agree. One story proves nothing. But one story can refute a general claim. The story of high-definition television refutes the claim that, without government assistance, America will lose all new technologies to her better financed foreign rivals. But it also refutes a more important claim. Remember when you went to Frank Bates and asked for protection from Japanese televisions?"

"Sure."

"One of your arguments was that if America lost its television industry, it would lose many future breakthroughs to the Japanese."

"Seemed reasonable at the time."

"Perhaps. I suspect self-interest may have interfered with your objectivity. But it was a common enough argument even among the disinterested. The same argument was made for high-definition television."

"And why not, Dave? It still seems like a reasonable argument."

"Don't you see? An America without a Frank Bates presidency is open to foreign trade and loses the television industry. But America still develops the best high-definition television system despite a late start and no government subsidy. Evidently, your argument about televisions was wrong. Even without an indigenous television industry, America can still compete in developing new technology."

"At least with high-definition television. But you don't know that there might be some products that are essential to developing future breakthroughs."

"I grant you that, Dave. There also might *not* be any such products. The case of high-definition television doesn't prove my case. But again, it is one piece of evidence that contradicts the possibility you mention."

"I don't know, Dave. It seems to me that new technologies are a special case because of the risk involved."

"New technology is inherently risky, Ed. Who bears that risk most effectively, the company and its stockholders, or the taxpayer?"

"There must be times you can make the case for the taxpayer. America as a whole gets many of the benefits, Dave."

"But America as a whole gets those benefits in most cases even if the Japanese, say, get the technology first. American consumers still get the product. America might not get the jobs in that industry. But what is to stop America from entering the industry once it gets started?"

"You gave the answer yourself. What if there is only room for one firm? Isn't it better for America if that one firm is American?"

"It will be better for the workers in that one firm. Not much of a case can be made that it is better for Americans in general. Besides, I await a real world example of this one firm that is so often discussed. The only case I know of is the Concorde. France and Britain together control the market for quick trips around the world. This market supremacy has not led to great wealth for France or Britain. You would be hard-pressed to find another case where the market for a technology was so narrow that there was only room for a single producer and where government intervention would determine which firm got in the market first. But companies keep arguing for protection and government aid in the name of the public good."

CHAPTER ELEVEN

Fair Trade vs. Free Trade

"But, Dave, what about the argument for a level playing field? If the other guy won't let our products into his country, why should we let his products into ours?"

"If your enemy cut off his nose, would you cut yours off out of fairness?"

"What?"

"If Japan or another nation keeps out American products, they are harming themselves. They are forcing their citizens to pay higher prices than necessary for the goods they consume. They are devoting unnecessary resources, people, raw materials, and capital to produce goods they could import at a lower cost. Should America impose the same costs on her citizens?"

"No, but it still isn't fair. If we're going to let Japanese companies sell here, they should let American companies sell there."

"Allow me to digress for a moment, Ed. How would you know if a foreign nation is keeping out American products?"

"They might have tariffs or quotas, I guess. Or they might have other barriers to imports that were harder to observe."

"OK. So how would you know if, overall, they were treating American products fairly?"

"I don't know. I guess you could look at the overall trade patterns between the two nations."

"If you and I are going to discuss the issue of fair trade, we have to consider a world where America imports something. In 1992, for example, in the America without a Frank Bates presidency, America imported about 3 million cars and trucks from Japan, while Japan imported about 14,000 cars and trucks from Chrysler, Ford, and GM."

"See! That's exactly my point. Something unfair must have been going on."

"Perhaps. Let's look a little more closely. How many oranges does Minnesota import from Florida in a given year?"

"I don't know. A lot."

"How many oranges do you think Florida imports from Minnesota?"

"Zero."

"Isn't that unfair, Ed? Shouldn't Florida help out Minnesota by importing just as many oranges from Minnesota as Minnesota imports from Florida?"

"But that doesn't make any sense, Dave. Minnesota doesn't *produce* any oranges."

"But they could, you know. They could build greenhouses and heat them year-round if necessary and have a huge orange crop. Of course, Minnesota oranges would be very expensive. One suspects the citizens of Florida would rather eat their home-grown oranges at a lower price. But that wouldn't stop the orange producers of Minnesota from demanding that Floridians eat Minnesota oranges in the name of fairness. Or worse, that the producers of Florida oranges use air-conditioning in their fields to make sure that there was a level playing field for the orange producers in both states."

"That's a misleading example, Dave. Cars and oranges aren't the same."

"You are right. But the example shows the stupidity of looking at unequal trade flows as inherently unfair. Trade flows *should be* unequal for any one product. It would make no sense for Japan and the United States to have equal trade flows in every good. The essence of trade is specialization. Of course, with cars, trade could flow in both directions, because unlike oranges, cars from Japan and America can differ by many attributes."

"So why did Japan import so few American cars?"

"The automobile executives of America would speak about how difficult it was to export a car to Japan. Japan had severe safety regulations. American automobile executives claimed that Japan used these and other regulations to raise the cost of selling American cars in Japan."

"Did they?"

"Perhaps. I am sure that there were some unpleasant hoops to leap through. Of course America had similar if not worse hurdles for Japanese cars. American anti-pollution laws were rather complex. Yet the Japanese designed anti-pollution devices for cars sold in America that complied with American laws and sometimes the laws of a particular state, such as California."

"You're implying a different explanation."

"I am, though certainly the Japanese government made it hard to sell some American products in Japan. But one deterrent to American automobile exports was the fault of American manufacturers. Japanese drive on the left side of the road, not the right. If you drive on the left-hand side of the road, the steering wheel should be placed on the right-hand side. Yet,

American cars manufactured for the Japanese market had their steering wheels where Americans like them, on the left. Can you imagine what would happen if Japanese manufacturers exported cars to America with steering wheels on the right-hand side of the car and then complained that Americans wouldn't buy the cars that sold perfectly well in Japan?"

"Why didn't American manufacturers make cars with steering wheels on the right-hand side for the Japanese market?"

"They started talking about it in 1993. So maybe they will at some point in the future."

"If Japan made it hard for American manufacturers to sell there, the limited sales might not have made up for the costs of switching the steering wheels."

"An excellent point, Ed. It's possible. European manufacturers in 1992 sold over 140,000 vehicles in Japan, ten times the American total. Many of them had the steering wheel on the correct side for Japanese roads. But it's possible that even this volume would not be sufficient to make the re-tooling profitable for American manufacturers. Or perhaps American manufacturers were not eager to sell many cars in Japan."

"How could that make sense?"

"The strategy was political. What they really wanted was protection in their home market, America. After all, in the early 90s, the American automobile market was over three times the size of the Japanese. Rather than fight for sales in Japan, it might have been more profitable to offset the inroads of Japanese companies in America. Poor sales in Japan allowed American manufacturers to complain about the Japanese market. Why? To justify retaliatory tariffs or quotas in the American market."

"Clever. But weren't there some cases where unfair business practices were a genuine barrier to American products selling in foreign markets?"

"Yes. Japan, for example, limited the entry of many American products and services. The government controlled certain contracts and favored Japanese companies. They limited entry into certain fields. Some Japanese companies refused to deal with foreign companies even, it is alleged, when they offered cheaper prices and higher quality. Legal restrictions, Japanese culture, and government policy all played a role in limiting U.S. sales in Japan."

"So Japanese policies were unfair."

"I don't know what 'unfair' means, Ed. If you mean that for some, and perhaps many, products, Japanese companies had easier access to Japanese consumers than did American companies, then Japanese policies were unfair. Such barriers, natural and imposed, exist everywhere. Meanwhile, in 1992, as I told you before, Japanese policies didn't stop the average Japanese citizen from importing more from the United States than the average American imported from Japan."

"But, Dave. You admit that Japan's playing field was unlevel for some American products. Shouldn't the American government have done something about it?"

"It depends. 'Fair trade' or 'leveling the playing field' are usually code words announcing an attack on the consumer. Take charges of dumping."

"I thought you told me that it was irrational to sell below cost."

"Usually it is. Unfortunately, in the America with imports that we visited earlier, the U.S. Department of Commerce had a broader definition of dumping than selling below cost. The Department of Commerce ruled that a foreign producer was dumping anytime his price in the United States was below the price in his home market. The implication was that he was selling below cost in the United States."

"It could be true, couldn't it, Dave?"

"It's conceivable, but unlikely for reasons we discussed before. Prices can differ in two markets for plenty of innocent reasons: because of short-run currency fluctuations or differing market conditions. Measured price differences do not imply a predatory motive. The Department of Commerce was uninterested in such issues, however. Acting at the behest of U.S. companies trying to handicap foreign competitors, the Department of Commerce simply compared the two prices."

"Seems straightforward."

"It was not. The Department of Commerce took the average price in the foreigner's home market over the preceding six months. If virtually any of the transactions in America took place below that average, even if the average U.S. price was above the average foreign price, the foreign producer was guilty of dumping. Normal market fluctuations in the price of the good or the exchange rate could then easily lead to a judgment of dumping. The Department of Commerce made numerous other arbitrary decisions in measuring quality and other aspects of the good. Politics pushed them toward a finding of dumping when none was actually there."

"Can you prove they were biased, Dave?"

"Between 1986 and 1992, the Department of Commerce ruled on 251 cases of alleged dumping. They found evidence of dumping in 97% of the cases."

"That does seem rather high. What happened after the Department of Commerce found the foreign producer guilty?"

"The United States International Trade Commission, or ITC, then determined whether U.S. competitors were harmed by the low prices. The ITC found such harm in 68% of the cases between 1986 and 1992 where the Department of Commerce found dumping. "

"What happened to the producer found guilty of dumping?"

"An antidumping fine was imposed for each unit sold. The amount of the fine was equal to the difference between the 'fair' price, as calculated by the Department of Commerce, and the price in America."

"So it's like a tariff."

"Very much so. For example, if the 'fair' price was judged to be $8, and the item sold for $6 in the United States, the foreign producer would have to pay $2 for every unit sold in the United States. It acted like a 33% tariff. The average fine at the end of the 1980s was over 50% of the United States price. You can see how an antidumping order encouraged foreigners to raise their prices to avoid the fines. The consumer was harmed in the name of 'fairness.' Between 1985 and 1989, over fifty different products were hit with antidumping fees or countervailing duties, a similar fine. The average American citizen at the time would conclude that dumping was a common economic phenomenon, when in fact, it may never have occurred."

"But some of those cases could have been actual dumping, Dave."

"Highly unlikely. Here is my favorite example. It is not atypical, particularly for goods coming from communist countries. Poland was once accused of dumping electric golf carts into the United States market. There were no sales of golf carts in Poland. Hard to believe there was dumping going on, but the Department of Commerce had to make a ruling. What did they do? There was no price in Poland to use as the 'fair' price. In such cases, the Department of Commerce finds a nation whose economy is similar to Poland's. They chose Canada. They compared the price of Canadian-made golf carts sold in Canada to the price of Polish-made golf carts sold in the U.S."

"You mean they didn't use the price that the Polish manufacturer charged in Canada?"

"No. They used the price a *Canadian* manufacturer charged there and assumed it equaled what the Polish firm would have charged in Poland."

"Seems a bit of a stretch."

"Agreed. But lo and behold, dumping was discovered using this creative definition. A few years later, the decision was re-opened. This time, the government didn't use Canada."

"Why not?"

"Who knows? Could it be because if you used Canada, there would be no violation? Instead, the Department of Commerce took a different approach, which is allowed by the law, called 'constructed value.' It involved constructing an estimate of cost, then adding on 8% for profit to get at what the price would be in the foreigner's home market."

"How did they estimate the cost?"

"As you can imagine, there is a wide range of estimates you can come up with, depending on how you deal with overhead and numerous other issues. The 8% is purely arbitrary and rather changes the concept of selling below cost. For products from communist countries it was even more creative. Because Poland is a communist country, wages and other prices are set artificially, instead of by the market. Using Polish wage rates might lead to low estimated costs, a low estimated Polish price, and no finding of dumping. So the Department of Commerce used Spanish wage rates."

"Spanish? Why Spanish?"

"I know it's hard to believe, but again, it's purely arbitrary. A foreign producer who wanted to avoid being charged with dumping, and filling out a 100 page questionnaire in English, then being hit with a potentially massive fine, had no idea in advance which country would be chosen. Here is another example—Chinese manhole covers sold in the United States. The Department of Commerce looked at the price of Belgian, Japanese, Canadian, and French manhole covers made in those countries to determine the 'Chinese' domestic price. The result was an 11% fee on Chinese manhole covers coming into the United States. So China raised its prices to avoid the penalty. A few years later, the case was re-opened and China was hit with a 97% fee, assessed retroactively."

"How did the fee jump to 97%?"

"Instead of using the cost of manhole covers in other nations, the Department of Commerce arbitrarily decided to use the 'estimated cost' measure of Chinese price. But, of course, they didn't use actual Chinese wage rates and costs of raw materials. That might lead to a low price and no finding of dumping. They used costs from the Philippines, where wages are nice and high. It made the price China charged in the United States look very low. You can imagine what such rulings did to the incentives of foreign producers to compete on price."

"It seems like an extraordinarily unfair way to deal with allegations of unfair trade."

"Now you can understand why the Department of Commerce so often found foreigners guilty of dumping. And why a guilty verdict rarely implied selling below cost."

"It's hard to believe the process was so arbitrary, Dave."

"I know. If we had time, we could look up case after case."

"Well, there must have been some times when the Department of Commerce found a case of dumping where a foreign seller actually sold at a price less than cost."

"It's possible. Very unlikely, and even then, beneficial to the consumer. But suppose a foreign producer really was selling below cost and you wanted to stop such behavior. Do you see why a law against dumping, even a well-intentioned one, is so likely to backfire? Implementing such a law is in the hands of the politicians. Instead of fairness, you get a world where the Department of Commerce uses arbitrary procedures and finds dumping 97% of the time. Ultimately, the consumer is the loser. By the way, there was another insidious effect of American antidumping law."

"What was that, Dave?"

"Turnabout was fair play. Other nations countered American law with antidumping statutes of their own, modeled on the U.S. law. For example, Monsanto sold Nutrasweet, a low-calorie sweetener, in Europe and the United States. Nutrasweet was protected by a patent, but the patent ran out in Europe before it ran out in the United States. Monsanto faced competition in Europe. Guess where the price of Nutrasweet was lower."

"Europe. Monsanto had competitors there."

"Correct. But because the price in Europe was lower than in the United States, European countries imposed a 75% antidumping fee, or tariff, on Nutrasweet sold in Europe, even though Monsanto was selling well above cost in both markets. Monsanto built a Nutrasweet factory in Europe, not because it made economic sense, but just to avoid the 75% fee. The European producers of Nutrasweet substitutes got rich at the expense of European consumers, and the world got poorer as less trade occurred."

"OK, Dave, I see how laws against dumping are a pretty costly way to 'level the playing field.' Is there a better way to deal with the barriers put up by foreign nations?"

"Antidumping laws level the playing field by raising barriers everywhere. Total trade falls and the world gets poorer. An alternative is to level the playing field by *lowering* barriers everywhere and moving toward freer trade. This was the mission of the General Agreement on Tariffs and Trade or GATT as it is called. GATT had the nations of the world sit down and reduce tariffs and quotas en masse. Then there were often auxiliary agreements such as the North American Free Trade Agreement, or NAFTA, which would create a regional free trade zone between Canada, Mexico, and the United States."

"The United States and Canada seem pretty similar, Dave. But Mexico? Didn't people worry about the U.S. losing jobs to low-wage Mexican workers from a free trade agreement with Mexico?"

"Indeed they did. Just as Americans were afraid of losing jobs to the Japanese back in 1960. In 1960, Japanese wages were a fraction of American wages, just as Mexican wages were in 1990."

"Mexico is a lot more convenient than Japan, Dave. Wouldn't American firms move their factories to Mexico to take advantage of cheap Mexican labor if there were no tariffs on Mexican goods coming into the United States?"

"Some did so without a trade agreement. But most American factories stayed where they were. The average American worker is much more skilled and productive than the average Mexican worker. Just because Japan or Mexico has lower wages than the United States does not mean that labor costs are lower there."

"It makes sense that one highly skilled worker can outperform a number of low-wage workers. I guess it would depend on the magnitude of the skill and wage differences."

"That is correct, Ed. The question is what actually happens when two economies with differing wage rates and skill levels interact."

"And?"

"Earlier, we saw what happened with the United States and Japan between 1960 and 1990. Japan gained some manufacturing jobs that America lost. But America was still able to create more jobs at higher wages than existed before. Of course, the gains to Americans were not equally distributed across all types of workers. The same thing happened when America began to trade more intensely with Mexico. American workers closest in skills to Mexican workers were the low-skill Americans. They found the demand for their services falling as factories moved to Mexico. They were harmed by Mexican competition, just as some of your workers were harmed by Japanese competition back in the 1960s."

"I bet they didn't like a trade bill that would intensify such changes."

"They didn't. Let me show you how strange the politics became. Have you ever been to a town in Illinois called Clearview?"

"Sure. It's a couple hours east of Star."

"That's right. Population about 25,000, and most of the people there worked in one of two factories. Both of those factories made brooms. In 1993, the workers in those plants made between six and ten dollars an hour. Those wages were well below the national average, but as in the case of your production line workers, it was a decent wage for people with at best, a high school diploma. The owners of these factories and their workers were particularly upset about the North American Free Trade Agreement."

"Why?"

"Because even without a Frank Bates presidency, as we have seen, there would still be some trade restrictions in the United States. Foreign brooms coming into the United States were hit with a 32% tariff. Even with that handicap, America imported a lot of brooms from Mexico. Eliminating that tariff would destroy a lot of jobs in Clearview."

"Don't you feel bad for those workers, Dave? Clearview is not a rich town. What would those people do if the broom jobs disappeared?"

"I do feel bad for them, Ed. It is some consolation that the tariffs would be reduced over a period of fifteen years. That gave some protection to the broom workers. And just as we saw in Star, the children of those workers would not presume that they could work in those factories after high school. They would have to find work elsewhere. Or go on to college to acquire more flexible and complex skills. America should not want broom-making jobs. They were called manufacturing jobs, but you can see that at $8 an hour, it took the average worker in Clearview almost a week to earn enough to buy a television, when the average American was working only three days to earn one. America was better off sending broom-making jobs to Mexico and getting cheap brooms from there."

"But, Dave. You can't expect those workers to favor free trade. Or their managers or bosses."

"No. They would be harmed. But their children would be harmed if America insisted on keeping low-skill jobs such as broom manufacturing. It is not surprising that short-run concerns are paramount, however. The owners of the broom factories made many trips to Washington, just as you did once, to try to save the jobs and wages of their workers. By the way, did you ever notice anything strange about Clearview when you were there?"

"Just that there were a lot of Mexican restaurants. We'd stop and have lunch there if the family was taking a car trip that took us through town."

"Do you know why Clearview has so many Mexican restaurants? One day, the owner of one of those factories went down to Mexico looking for broomwinders, people who could 'wind' a broom, part of the assembly process. A lot of those Mexicans came to Clearview and stayed. They wrote their relatives and told them to come to America. Wages were a lot higher in Clearview than they were back in Mexico. By 1990, half of the workers in those factories were either born in Mexico, or were the children of parents born there."

"That is pretty strange, Dave."

"Here is the irony. Americans who opposed NAFTA were worried about jobs migrating to Mexico when tariffs were lowered. But in a strange sense, a lot of the jobs were already gone even when brooms were protected by a tariff. There is little difference between a factory in Mexico making brooms, and a factory in Clearview using Mexican labor to make brooms. Without the protection of tariffs, those jobs would probably never have been in America in the first place. In the meanwhile, with tariffs in place, Americans paid more for brooms. The Mexican immigrants, their American co-workers, and the owners of the firms profited at the consumer's expense."

"Well, Dave, I can understand why free trade agreements are controversial. Are they successful in promoting trade?"

"In practice, they are not as effective as they look on paper. Even GATT allowed antidumping fees to be assessed when pricing was judged to be 'unfair.' However, most observers believed GATT was a success. World trade increased many-fold during the time of these agreements."

"Is there another way to level the playing field while encouraging more trade, Dave?"

"A favorite is to threaten foreign nations with some form of retaliation if they do not lower their trade barriers."

"Does it work?"

"I cannot think of a single example. Barriers do not exist because of some persuasive economic theory arguing they are good for the nation. They are in place to enrich domestic producers. Remember the case of Japanese rice? The Japanese political system gives a disproportionate weight to votes from rural areas. So Japanese rice producers have an inordinate amount of power. Will the threat of tariffs on Japanese automobiles encourage the Japanese government to allow rice imports from America? The threat does not reduce the political power of Japanese rice producers in the Japanese parliament. Ask yourself, Ed, how Americans would feel if the Japanese threatened America in a similar fashion."

"But if the carrot of mutual tariff and quota reduction doesn't work, what can a nation do to reduce trade barriers?"

"You do what's best for your own citizens and open your markets to products from all over the world. If Japan won't let in American rice or even American cars, as it is alleged, then ignore them. Allow their cars into America free of tariff and in any number. Give the American consumer cheap cars. America will become wealthy and the rest of the world will notice. This is precisely the policy my nation, England, followed with great success in the nineteenth century."

"But you may as well use the *threat* of imposing a tariff to get foreign nations to reduce their tariffs."

"Perhaps. If the threat is effective. After some point, a threat that is never carried out is no longer credible. If you want to maintain credibility, eventually you have to carry out the threat and impose tariffs in the name of opening the markets of your trading partners."

"Is that so bad?"

"Yes, if it fails to affect foreign trade barriers and only ends up hurting American consumers. Moreover, I find it hard to take the motivation seriously. The *possibility* that a tariff will encourage foreigners to reduce their barriers allows the protectionist politician to have his cake and eat it too. Take a Congressman whose home district is in Michigan or Missouri where a lot of auto plants are located. Such a member of Congress is invariably a protectionist, trying to raise the wages of the workers in his district."

"That's his job, isn't it?"

"I can't say. By helping one group of his constituents, he harms the larger, but more diffused interests of his constituents who buy cars. This would bother me less if the politician were more candid. But call him a protectionist and you will be greeted with a look of shock and horror. 'Me a protectionist? You wrong me, sir. I favor free trade. But I also favor fair trade. Let the other nations of the world practice free trade and we will join them. In fact we'll encourage them to take the path of free trade. We'll punish them with tariffs until they get rid of their own. Not to enrich the special interests of the manufacturer and the automobile worker who contribute to my campaign and who vote for me. Oh, no. Patriotism is my motivation. And to encourage the rest of the nations to see the light.' Thus is self-interest cloaked in patriotism and altruism for propaganda purposes. There is no evidence that such schemes are effective in lowering the barriers of other nations. They mainly keep wages in Missouri and Michigan higher than they would be otherwise."

"It does sound like Alice-in-Wonderland to call yourself a free-trader while always voting for tariffs."

"Such members of Congress have other excuses to salvage their public image. They will tell you that free trade works fine 'in theory.' Or that free trade only works if the rest of the world follows free trade. These are rhetorical arguments to cover the smell of narrow self-interest."

"Is there any truth to the idea that free trade only works if everyone follows it?"

"Why should there be? Why should the benefits from free trade to America require an assumption that all nations follow free trade? Let me make it very simple. Suppose Japan refuses to allow American televisions into Japan. America can accept or refuse to accept Japanese products. Which is better for America? Unless the refusal of Japanese products causes them to change their policy, all you are doing is harming your citizens because the Japanese government sees fit to harm its own."

"But what about the overall balance of trade? If, for example, Japan makes it hard for American products to sell in Japan, won't America run a deficit with Japan? Even if Japan imports a lot of pharmaceuticals and airplanes from the United States, does that make up for the cars and rice they don't import?"

"Not always. Remember that trade restrictions tend to reduce the volume of both imports and exports. So there need not be a relationship between Japanese restrictions and a surplus or a deficit. In 1992, in a world where America allows imports, the United States had a trade deficit of $50 billion dollars with Japan."

"Fifty billion! Good grief!"

"Yes, it scared a lot of people then too."

"I can understand why. Isn't that clearly a sign that something was wrong?"

"The answer would depend on the reason for the trade deficit. There are many destructive ways to fix it. One way to improve America's deficit with Japan would have been to make the United States a less attractive place to invest."

"Sounds like a bad mistake."

"Oh, it would have been. But it would have helped reduce the measured deficit with Japan. A fundamental reason the United States ran a trade deficit with Japan was because Japan had a higher savings rate than America and America had more opportunities for investment than Japan."

"What did that have to do with the trade deficit?"

"Quite a bit, it turns out. If Japanese citizens wish to save a great deal of money and there are few good investment opportunities in Japan relative to America, some of their savings will end up as investments in America. Americans will use the yen from those investments to buy Japanese goods. So while the United States will be running a trade deficit with Japan, it will be running a surplus on the investment side. If this is the cause of the trade deficit, you can see how futile it is to try and manage the deficit by looking at specific products."

"What do you mean?"

"The trade deficit with Japan is calculated by adding up the deficits or surpluses between the United States and Japan for the various products they exchange with one another. The government looks at cars, and pharmaceuticals, and airplanes, and televisions, and beef, and so on, and calculates the deficit by examining each product and summing up the deficit or surplus to arrive at the overall deficit."

"Sounds straightforward."

"It is. Sort of. That $50 billion doesn't include services, an important surplus area for America of about $14 billion in 1992. But ignore that. And ignore that a nation's trade position vis-à-vis a single other nation is not very important in a world of many trading partners. Even if the deficit is calculated perfectly, the way the deficit is calculated leads to confusion."

"Why?"

"Suppose the overall deficit is $50 billion. Take the extreme case where the United States imports $25 billion worth of cars from Japan while selling none to Japan. So half of the deficit is due to cars. What happens if the United States bans the import of Japanese cars?"

"American car manufacturers will sell a lot more cars."

"Correct. Which is why they lobby for quotas in the name of reducing the deficit. Once again, self-interest masquerades as patriotism. But I was really asking what happens to the deficit."

"Come on, Dave. Are you asking me what happens to $50 billion if I subtract $25 billion? Is this a trick question?"

"Yes."

"OK, so the deficit doesn't get cut in half. Why not?"

"Ed, how many calories of food do you consume on a typical day?"

"I have no idea. What's that have to do with the trade deficit?"

"Humor me. If you wanted to calculate your caloric consumption, how would you do it?"

"I'd make a list of everything I ate on a typical day, and calculate the calories for each item and then add them all up."

"Exactly. Now suppose you found that potatoes accounted for 20% of the calories. If there were a potato shortage in your area and stores were not carrying any potatoes, would your calorie consumption fall by 20%?"

"If I couldn't get potatoes, I'd probably substitute rice or bread. Otherwise I'd be awfully hungry if my calorie consumption fell by 20%."

"America's appetite for Japanese products acts in a similar way. The government calculates the deficit by looking at each individual component or product. But the products are not independent. Many factors such as savings policy and government budget deficits fuel America's demand for Japanese products. Changing the amount imported of one product will have little effect on the overall deficit because of changes in purchases of other products. Similarly, some American manufacturers demand that the Japanese set minimum targets for imports of the American product. While such targets may help the manufacturer, they will have little or no effect on the overall deficit. They are like assuming that if you were forced to eat an extra slice of bread a day that you will gain weight. You won't, if you cut back somewhere else."

"I understand the point about appetite and calories. What I don't understand is why variables such as government deficit and savings determine the trade deficit independently of the individual components."

"I'm afraid that will take a long time to explain."

"Then let's talk about something that should be a little bit simpler. Can you tell me why everyone is driving Ford Fairlanes and Chevy Impalas?"

CHAPTER TWELVE

Self-Sufficiency Is the Road to Poverty

"Ed, this is the world where Frank Bates becomes President in 1960 and gets a bill passed so that America allows no imports. You are looking at an America after 35 years of self-sufficiency. Let me remind you of the sequence of events. It started with the quota on Japanese imports of televisions. When people saw how your workers prospered, they wanted protection for their industries. Usually such efforts fail. I have been given the power to let you see what would happen if such efforts succeeded and all foreign products were banned."

"Dave, I understand the power of free trade now. What I don't understand is why a world of no trade is so bad. After all, self-sufficiency is a virtue. It's better to be self-sufficient than to depend on others."

"It would appear that way. But self-sufficiency is the road to poverty. You told me you don't grow your own corn. But you could at least imagine it. How about making your own shirt? How long would it take you to grow your own cotton, spin it into thread, and weave your own cloth? You would be self-sufficient. Wouldn't it be better to depend on the cotton farmer, the thread spinner, the cloth weaver? Is it not clear that to make your own shirts and shoes and grow your own food is to lead a life of bitter poverty?"

"OK, but you're taking a good idea to a ridiculous extreme. Just because it's hard to be completely self-sufficient doesn't mean it's a bad idea to be a little self-sufficient."

"I agree, Ed. It usually is good to be a little self-sufficient. It is also good to 'depend' on others. Neither is a virtue in its own right as long as you define your terms correctly. When you buy shirts from a department store, you're dependent on a long chain of people beginning with the farmer in Egypt, perhaps, who grew the cotton, down to the owner of the department store. But is there anything negative about this dependency? You and the others in the chain benefit from your purchase of the shirt. It surely is superior to growing your own cotton and doing all the other steps yourself."

"I understand that in the case of an individual. But why should it apply to nations? What's it have to do with all these Ford Fairlanes everyone is driving?"

"Remember when you got that bill passed banning imports of Japanese televisions?"

"I guess that was an extreme version of a quota."

"Right. Remember how all your workers got rich?"

"Sure. I realize now that some of that wealth was illusory."

"Not to them. Their wealth was real. Those were real cars they were able to buy, and real vacations they were able to take. They did not know of the wealth lost to others. What was illusory was assuming that the gains your workers experienced were the total effect of the quota. The total impact on America was negative when you included the harm to consumers."

"But, Dave. You told me before they were driving Corvettes and Cadillacs. How did those cars turn into Ford Fairlanes?"

"Other industries followed yours in asking for protection from foreign competition. What was good for television workers must be good for those in automobiles, and textiles, and every product. President Bates proposed a bill forbidding all imports."

"Was there any opposition to the bill?"

"Oh sure. A bunch of economists took out an ad in *The New York Times* calling it a disaster. But people have always made fun of economists. Call them slippery and charlatans and every other name in the book. Some of those insults are deserved. But economists are pretty unanimous about free trade. People didn't listen. Congress passed the bill and President Bates signed it. It was hailed as a landmark in American history. And it was."

"What happened then?"

"Not much, at first. But slowly, changes took place. Without imports to put dollars in the hands of foreigners, industries that relied on exports faltered or collapsed. Remember that movie your grandson was watching, *Aladdin*?"

"Sure. I liked it quite a bit myself."

"It never got made. Disney stopped making new films in the early 1980s."

"Why?"

"Exports were a significant share of their profits. Without those profits, Disney didn't have the incentive to hire enough cartoonists and designers to make new movies. They just show their old films now."

"That's a shame. I liked that movie."

"Disney was one of many companies that never grew to their full potential. Other companies never even came into existence. For example, Bill Gates is a car mechanic. He—"

"Who's Bill Gates?"

"Sorry. Bill Gates would have been a billionaire in the 1990s in a world of free trade. Without free trade he leads a modest life tinkering with cars."

"Is it so bad if we lose a billionaire and gain a regular Joe making a modest living?"

"It probably doesn't thrill Bill Gates. But the real loss is America's. You only see one man's income being lower. The real loss is the industry he helped transform, computer software, and the products that he brought to market. Those products made him rich. But they also enriched the lives of millions of others. He started a company called Microsoft. Its products would have been used all over America and the world if there had been free trade."

"But, Dave, he could still sell the product in America, couldn't he? Aren't there enough Americans who can buy innovative products?"

"There are many Americans to buy his products. But without imports and the roundabout way of production, America cannot have everything she enjoyed with free trade. To make Microsoft a great company, Bill Gates needed the skills of countless programmers, marketers, and distributors of his product. There are a limited number of those people to go around. Motorola, and Procter & Gamble, and Boeing, and Disney, and Apple, and Microsoft are all competing for those talented people."

"But why are there plenty of them in a world of free trade and not enough in a world of self-sufficiency? Isn't the population the same in both cases?"

"The population is the same. But the jobs being done by the working-age members of that population are not."

"But if Motorola and those other companies have high-paying jobs, why won't the talented people end up there under self-sufficiency?"

"When America stopped allowing imports, certain vital products were no longer available from overseas."

"For example?"

"Oil. Textiles. Shoes. Cars. Steel. Consumers turned to the American producers of these goods."

"That must have been good for those American producers."

"You might think so, the same way your workers and your company flourished when Americans were forced to buy your televisions instead of having Japanese televisions to choose from. But when every industry is in the same boat you don't get the same effect."

"Why not? And why was the overall effect on the economy so negative?"

"Think of it as the roundabout way to wealth wreaking vengeance. When your industry prospered, we talked before how consumers suffered more than television companies gained. Why was that?"

"Televisions got more expensive."

"Right. Consumers had to pay more for televisions. But there were other effects, as well. When the television industry expanded, it drew workers, capital, and raw materials away from other industries. America lost the goods that those industries would have produced using those. A single industry can expand and enrich itself at the expense of other industries and consumers. But not all industries can expand simultaneously. There are not enough workers to allow it. There is not enough capital. There are not enough raw materials."

"I understand the principle, Dave. I just don't see why it has to be that way. You say there are not enough workers to go around. But all the workers who used to make exports will now be available to produce the imports."

"That's right, but there was a reason to produce the goods the roundabout way rather than the direct way. America gets poorer producing everything the direct way. When the television industry benefited at the expense of others, the harm to the country as a whole was spread thin so it was effectively hidden. When every industry pursues protection, the impoverishment of the country is out in the open."

"I don't see why it has to happen, Dave."

"Think about all the goods America used to import that she will now have to produce on her own. Take all the steel and all the cars and all the watches and all the calculators and all the wool and all the cotton and all the sugar and all the coffee and all the rest. Stack them to the sky. How was America able to enjoy all of those goods under free trade?"

"The roundabout way?"

"The roundabout way. Under free trade, all over America, workers and machines make many goods the roundabout way. By making things Brazilians want and trading them for coffee and shoes. By selling pharmaceuticals and airplanes to Japan and trading them for calculators and video players. Use your mind's eye to put those workers, their factories, and their machines all in one place. In one giant industrial park are all the chemists and the aerospace engineers and marketers and distribution people and the factories and offices they work in. They are the real resources America uses to get imported goods. Imagine them all gathered together."

"I see them."

"When America stops importing, all of those people are going to have to make the watches and the shoes and all of the other products America used to import. They will have to produce the 2,000,000 cars that used to come from Japan. They are going to have to grow the cotton and the coffee and bring the oil out of the ground that used to come from abroad."

"OK."

"Go to the gate of this enormous industrial park. Tell the order clerk:

'I want 2,000,000 cars and so many pounds of sugar and coffee and this many watches...' and so on. A year's worth of the goods that America imports. You tell the clerk you will be back in one year to pick up the goods. The clerk takes the order into the park. Do you think they will be able to fill the order?"

"Of course not. You can't expect chemists from Merck to be able to find oil or Boeing assemblers to be able to make cars in an airplane factory."

"True. Let's give them a chance. A miracle takes place. The machines from the airplane factory become an automobile assembly line. Take all the factories and turn them into factories for the things they need to make now."

"It's still impossible. The workers don't have the right skills."

"Let there be another miracle. That Merck chemist who now has to be in the oil business? Let him instantly have a degree in petroleum engineering with all of the knowledge he would have acquired in school. Let all the workers have the knowledge they would have acquired if they knew all along they were going to be in the watch business or the television business. Do you think they could fill the order?"

"I don't know. I would think so."

"They can't. It can't be done. The head of the park will find that no matter how he mobilizes the workers with their new found skills, he can't fill the order. He will have to bring new workers into the industrial park. Or build more factories there. Or bring in more machines to be used in new factories. The park will be booming. But it will be booming just to match the production of watches, cars, and so on, that America used to import. Meanwhile, outside of the park there are fewer workers and fewer machines available to produce everything else. So the total amount of goods America can enjoy must go down."

"How do you know that the workers inside the park can't fill the order without bringing in extra people and resources? Why won't there be enough land and factories and machines?"

"The roundabout way to wealth. Suppose Boeing sells 25 planes per year in Japan and it takes 10,000 workers at Boeing to make those planes. The revenue from those planes allows Americans to buy 200,000 cars from Japan. But it will take more than 10,000 workers of that skill level to make those 200,000 cars using the direct way, instead of the roundabout way."

"How do you know?"

"If it took fewer than 10,000 workers, then Boeing, or someone else, could produce $3 billion worth of cars with fewer workers. They'd make more profits making cars instead of planes. It is not because Americans are less skilled than the Japanese at making cars. They're just a lot better at making planes and that is a more efficient way to make cars."

"But American cars are just as good and just as cheap as foreign cars. Why can't American cars replace foreign cars just as cheaply and efficiently?"

"American cars *are* just as cheap and just as good as foreign cars. But this equality is misleading. Your wife Martha bakes her own bread now and then, doesn't she?"

"You bet, and it's better than you can buy in the store."

"If it's better than you can buy in the store, she must bake often. Does she ever buy bread in the store?"

"Sure, Dave. Baking bread takes a lot of time. It's not worth it to make it all the time. She bakes when she finds the time."

"So she imports bread into your household to go along with domestic production."

"You could call it that."

"Don't you see the paradox, Ed? If your wife's bread is better than she can buy in the store, isn't it irrational to buy some in the store? You just told me hers is better."

"It is. It's just that some days she's tired or busy."

"It may make sense to bake some of your own bread. But that doesn't imply that baking *all* the bread you eat is a good idea, even though the occasional home-baked loaf is better and cheaper than a store-bought loaf."

"Why not?"

"Think about how Martha and you would feel if the government banned the sale of bread and you were not allowed to 'import' bread into the economy called your household. Martha might shrug and say, 'It doesn't matter. My bread is just as good as store-bought, it's cheaper, and I even enjoy baking bread.' But suppose that to bake all of the family's bread, Martha must make multiple batches. She would find that the additional loaves she bakes would be much more expensive than the ones she used to buy. The money expended on the additional loaves is still less than the cost of store-bought bread. But for Martha to bake all of her household's bread is going to take a lot more time than when she baked occasionally. And the cost of that time is much higher."

"How can that be?"

"Because the true cost of the time spent baking is not monetary, but the lost activities Martha no longer enjoys because she is busy baking."

"You know what else, Dave? She probably wouldn't replace the lost store-bought bread loaf-for-loaf with her own homemade loaves."

"Why not, Ed?"

"When she bought the bread in the store, the cost was the same for each additional loaf. But you are right. Each homemade loaf gets more and more expensive as she has to give up additional activities in or outside of the house to do more baking. At first she gives up relatively unimportant activities. But as her time spent baking bread expands, the things she stops doing get more and more valuable. So we might not choose to eat as much bread as we used to. We'll be worse off. We'll have less bread and fewer shared activities."

"Bravo, Ed. I salute you. It is the same principle we discussed before when we talked about how in the face of a quota, domestic production will not expand enough to make up for lost imports."

"I see it now."

"And I hope you also see how the equality of price and quality of American goods and foreign-made goods does not imply that America can replace foreign imports without a cost."

"But why is the nation like a household? Why do cars get harder to make?"

"Imagine America having to start up new car factories with new workers in those factories with enough of both to make the 2,000,000 cars that used to come from Japan. To do so would mean drawing productive capacity and workers away from other industries. America would no longer enjoy what those workers used to make. But in addition, the workers in those factories producing an additional 2,000,000 cars couldn't be as productive as the workers making the first 2,000,000 cars made in America."

"Why not? Wouldn't they adopt the same technology?"

"They would, presumably. But the workers and managers would not execute the technology as artfully, efficiently, and cheaply as the people already doing it. The first 2,000,000 cars are made by those Americans with the strongest interest and skills to work in an automotive factory. The managers in those factories will be the best at motivating and leading those workers to productivity. As you open more and more factories with more and more workers, and more and more managers, you no longer get the best ones. You start attracting workers and managers who are less efficient than the ones initially attracted to the industry. It gets more and more expensive to make a car. Eventually, in the case of cars for America, it becomes cheaper to make cars the roundabout way via imports rather than produce more cars by opening car factories."

"I don't know, Dave. It seems like making a car is making a car. Can't anyone figure out the steps on the assembly line?"

"Doesn't everybody know how to throw a baseball in America?"

"Sure."

"Do you think the worst ten pitchers in professional baseball are just as good as the top ten?"

"No."

"It's the same way with working in an auto factory or running one. Some people are better than others. Some take orders better. Some give orders better. Take your television plant in Star. Did you just hire people at random because anyone can figure out how to assemble televisions? Were all your plant managers equally good at motivating workers?"

"No. But it's still not easy to understand."

"Think of it this way. In a world where imports are allowed, Honda Accord and Ford Taurus are similar cars selling at a similar price. This leads to the conclusion that American cars are just as good as Japanese cars. But this is only true at the current levels of production where America, because of imports, does not have to make all of her own cars domestically. Eliminating the option of the Honda Accord to the American consumer is going to cause the price of the Taurus to rise. A decrease in supply leads to an increase in price. Another way to see it is that an increase in the demand for American cars cannot be satisfied without a price increase. And now you should understand why. Ford can't afford to make up for the lost Accords without a higher price. It takes a higher price to make it worthwhile for Ford to replace even some of the lost Accords, and that is because of the higher costs of larger and larger plants and the higher costs of opening new plants."

"I see that, Dave."

"But that is only part of the story. The other fallacy in assuming that America does not need foreign supply is to believe that innovation will continue. Without imports, the Ford Fairlane would not have become the Taurus. And without the Accord to prod Ford today, the Taurus will never become whatever it can become in the next thirty years."

"It's still hard to understand how all the effects of no imports lead to such an overall loss in standard of living. I'm struggling to see all of the connections."

"Think of Martha baking all of that bread or even some of it. Think about what life would be like if you had to make your own everything. Your house would have less of everything because Martha's and your time is limited. If you are forced to make everything for yourself, your command over goods and services has to fall. America's house looks the same way when there are no imports."

"It's still kind of hard to see everything that's going on, Dave."

"Here is another way to see it. In international conflict, a nation will try to place an embargo on its enemy. Why? To impoverish the enemy. How? By cutting off its ability to interact with the rest of the world. Putting up tariffs and quotas, or in the extreme, deciding to be self-sufficient, is to place an embargo on oneself. Does that sound like a beneficial policy?"

"I guess not. But if I were alive in 1995, I think I'd still feel guilty if I were one of those Americans buying a car from the Japanese."

"Then you have learned nothing tonight. If you buy an American car, you are helping the American autoworker and the stockholder in American car companies. If you buy a Japanese car, you are helping the workers of Merck and Boeing and their stockholders and executives. You should buy the car you get the most pleasure from. The American auto manufacturer asks you to buy American so that America is not dependent on foreigners. But it is easy to keep Americans from buying foreign cars—make a higher quality product at a lower price. When the American manufacturer can't do it on his own, he asks the government to force out the Japanese cars or impose a 'voluntary' quota. The reduction in supply drives up the price of American cars as we talked about before. That increase in price is really a welfare payment. It's a handout imposed on the car buyer to help out the auto manufacturer. Talk about a failure to be self-sufficient."

"Take it easy, Dave, you're getting excited."

"In my condition, Ed, a heart attack is not a big worry. Why should guilt enter into a consumer's decision? If the Stellar Television Company made an inferior or overpriced television, would you expect people to keep buying your product because they felt sorry for you? Is that the road to genuine self-sufficiency? Genuine self-sufficiency is not demanded of others as an arbitrary rule, but earned. What do you think happens to productivity when a worker or firm knows that no matter how shoddy or poorly produced their product is, people will buy it out of guilt or pity? People should buy the products that give them the best value for the money."

"But, Dave, if America became so poor between 1960 and 1995 because imports were banned, why didn't people get rid of the laws that kept out foreign goods? Couldn't people see they were getting poorer?"

"Sure, but people were scared. They didn't blame protectionism for their poverty. When economists proposed re-opening America to the world, people worried about their jobs. What would replace the jobs they already had, if foreigners were allowed to compete? How would you vote if you were an engineer in the American oil industry in Louisiana, or a watchmaker in Massachusetts, or a worker in a textile mill in the Carolinas? Getting rid of quotas would cost you your job."

"But you argue that other jobs would arise to replace them."

"People couldn't see that. Not only did they fear the transition between the old world and the new, they couldn't imagine the computer chip or the portable computer or the pharmaceuticals yet to be discovered to fight disease. There were no industries like that even to imagine. People were content to hold on to what they had."

CHAPTER THIRTEEN

The Choice

"Dave, you've worn me out. Can I see how my kids turn out in an America without trade?"

"Of course. I do get a bit long-winded at times. It's the politician in me. Remember that your children's lives are going to be very different from how they were before. When we saw them before, Steven was running a computer software company and Susan was running manufacturing for The Limited. Their lives are going to be different."

"Why?"

"Because the world we are in now is the world where America is self-sufficient. The opportunities available to your children will not be the same."

"So how is Susan doing, Dave?"

"She's doing fine. She has three children, two girls and a boy. She is married to a fine man. They live in Star."

I took Ed to Susan's house. Susan never made it to graduate school. She never made it to Hong Kong. She spent her time raising her family. We watched as Susan put the kids to bed and finished cleaning up the kitchen.

"She looks pretty happy to me, Dave."

"I daresay she is. Far be it from me to argue that doing without foreign products makes you unhappy. Just poorer than you might otherwise be."

"There's nothing wrong with raising a family."

"Certainly not, Ed. The question is whether Susan should have the opportunity to choose a different life. In a world without imports, the choices she faces are more limited."

"How about Steven?"

"He's here in town, too. He's running the Stellar Television Company."

Steven lived in a nice house on a quiet street off of Main Street. We watched Steven helping his son Justin with his math homework. There was no big screen television, no voice controlled computer. Just a math book, a pad of yellow paper, and a dining room table.

"Why are Justin's glasses so thick, Dave?"

"Remember when we visited Justin before, his father wouldn't let him watch the movie for too long? He still can't watch much television. Too tough on his eyes. In the world of free trade, he controlled his eye problem with a drug Merck developed. They weren't able to develop that drug in a world without trade, so Justin wears glasses instead. The glasses work almost as well."

I didn't tell Ed, but the people Upstairs had given him a break. Without that Merck drug, Justin would have lost his eyesight entirely. But the people Upstairs thought that if Ed's grandson went blind under a world of no imports, Ed's choice about whether to support Frank Bates wouldn't be an exercise of free will. It's easy to love free trade if it can keep your grandson from going blind.

"Steven seems pretty happy too, Dave."

"He does seem to be. I can't allow you to talk to Steven. If you could, you could ask him what it is like working for the same company his father did, and his father before him."

"It was good enough for me."

"I know. But whether it is good enough for him is a more complicated issue. Think back to a boy in 1960 with his dreams. Now you only see the man."

"The man seems happy. And sure Star isn't as lively as it was under free trade and we don't have frozen yogurt or Circuit City or Wal-Mart. But I like Star the way it always was."

"I doubt it. You like the Star of 1960, but I doubt you'd like the Star of 100 years earlier when there was horse manure in the streets and children had rickets and women died in childbirth with much greater frequency. You like what you are used to. But I'll accept part of what you say. Money is not everything. Wealth is not everything. Nor is America with free trade a paradise. Free trade leads to more opportunity, more wealth, and a more dynamic world. But a more dynamic world does not benefit everyone."

"What happens under free trade to the people who are not creative, who can't go to college. What will they do, Dave?"

"There are still jobs for people without a college degree. There are just fewer jobs in manufacturing than there once were. When Federal Express creates 100,000 jobs, they're not all for MBAs. They have jobs across the entire spectrum of skills. But free trade hurts some people. So does protectionism. You saw what America looks like when there is self-sufficiency, when America keeps all the jobs."

"But maybe Frank Bates made a mistake. Maybe he shouldn't have banned the import of all goods, just high-wage goods. He should have allowed Americans to import coffee and cotton and crude oil, but kept the high-technology, high-skill, high-wage jobs in America."

"Ed. Don't look at the jobs. Look at the people. If Americans are good at flipping hamburgers because they have low skills, then they will end up flipping hamburgers. You can't turn a hamburger flipper into a computer software designer by banning imports of computer software and 'saving' those jobs for the hamburger flippers to take. Well, you can. But it will end up making America poorer, not richer. You can help a low-skill individual through protectionism by punishing other Americans with high prices. Is that fair?"

"I don't know."

"And ask yourself if it is wise. If a group of Americans do not compete well in the global marketplace because their skills are readily available around the globe, how should America respond? By protecting them and insulating them from the competition they face, or by encouraging them and their children to improve their skills? I hope you have learned tonight that the choice America faces is not between more jobs or fewer jobs. The real choice is between a static world and a dynamic world. A world of encouraging people to dream and encouraging them to acquire the skills to make those dreams come true and a world of encouraging people to be content with what they have and to dream less."

"Which is better, Dave?"

"That is for you to decide. I will leave you with one thought. In the Bible, in the Book of Deuteronomy, God addresses the Israelites and tells them: 'I have set before you life and death, a blessing and a curse. Choose life.' Many Biblical commentators have asked why God implores or commands the Israelites to choose life. What kind of a choice is there between life and death? It's no choice. It's obvious you should choose life. So why does God demand the obvious? Perhaps God was not referring to a literal choice between life and death, but a spiritual choice between experiencing life versus fearing life's experiences and running away from them. Choose life, Ed."

"But which life, Dave. They both look inviting, I—. Hey! Dave! Dave! Dave!"

I was gone. My time was up and Ed was on his own, back in his den in 1960 in Star, Illinois. Frank Sinatra was still pouring his heart out on the hi-fi. Martha slept in the next room. Steven and Susan were children, sleeping the sleep of children, down the hall. Down the road, the Stellar Television Company was locked up for the night awaiting another day of production. Televisions were the only product in America where foreign competition was completely banned. Epcot Center and Disneyworld were a gleam in Walt's eye. There were no personal computers. No frozen yogurt. No VCRs. No *Aladdin*. No Federal Express. No Wal-Mart. No Circuit City. They hung in the balance of time, unrealized.

Ed sat stunned for quite some time, staring at the piece of chocolate cake and the glass of milk that still sat on the table in the den as fresh as when we left them, worlds ago. Ed finally drifted off to sleep....

"Honey, wake up! You've got to make that speech for Frank Bates in Los Angeles. You'll miss your plane."

"Martha!"

"Ed, why did you sleep out here? I'll help you pack. You better jump in the shower."

Ed didn't say much. Martha wasn't surprised. She knew Ed had a lot on his mind. She just didn't know how much.

Ed made his plane to Los Angeles for the convention. He took his speech with him, the same one Frank Bates had sent him, nominating Frank for President. As I looked on from Upstairs, my heart sank, but I did not despair. I knew there was still time.

On July 14, 1960, at 11:00 a.m. on a breezy Los Angeles day, a taxi pulled up to the front doors of the Beverly Wilshire Hotel, and Ed Johnson stepped out. He checked in, headed to his room, and told the hotel operator to hold all calls and wake him at 4:00 P.M. He slept soundly. A good or a bad sign, I did not know.

Ed rose, showered, and put on a clean shirt and a suit. He took a taxi to Santa Monica and the beach. He walked along the beach for an hour, then found a bench in a grassy park, looking out over the water that separates the two great economies of the post-war era, Japan and the United States. He sat there for a while, watching the earth spin forward and bring the sun down into the ocean. Then he caught a taxi to the Sports Arena where the convention was being held. He still had his speech with him. I was not encouraged.

Time passed slowly for both Ed and me. The crowd was an undulating mass of banners, buttons, and placards. The Frank Bates supporters had their share of signs: Put America First; Free Trade is Unfair Trade; Protect American Jobs—Keep Out Foreign Products. And my favorite: If Americans Buy Foreign Products, Where Will Our Children Work? Finally Ed's turn came. He was to make a key nominating speech for Frank Bates. The journalists were ready. The television cameras were ready. Now Ed was ready and he began to speak.

He read from the speech he had brought, the one Frank Bates's staff put together. He spoke of Frank Bates and the success of the Stellar Television Company. He spoke of Star, his home town, and what makes Star special. It was really what makes every small town in America special. The open hearts of its people. The simplicity. The constancy of life. It's a good life, and Ed described it well.

You could feel the pride of the people listening. Many were from Chicago and Los Angeles and New York City, but their pride in small town America was real.

"In my home town of Star, the rough edges of life are smoothed by the familiar. You know your neighbors because you've lived next door to them for years. Your friends are friends for life, and your family is there to share good times and bad. My father was born in Star, founded Stellar Television Company, and died there. I was born in Star and will live there till I die. My children were born there, and they too will likely die there."

At that line, Ed hesitated and looked lost for a moment. I could hear him repeat the line to himself, "My children were born there, and they too will likely die there." I wondered if he was seeing Susan in Hong Kong, or Steven, running his own company out in California.

Ed took a deep breath. I took one too. There wasn't much time left. When Ed started to speak again, he put his speech aside and looked straight out at the crowd.

"I don't come often to Los Angeles. I'm always a little bit uneasy before I arrive. It's noisier and faster. It's different from Star, and change is always threatening. But after a few days, I usually feel at home in Los Angeles or Chicago or New York. Not enough to want to stay, but enough to understand why so many of you choose to live here. Noisier and faster, yes, but something else as well. There's more life here.

"Of course, we have our share of excitement down in Star. A new film comes to the Bijou every month. Even in Star, and in all the small towns across America, we have our dreamers and achievers, our people who yearn to remake the world. In Star, it might be a young boy who dreams of running his own factory. In another town and place, a girl hears the lonely whistle of a train and dreams of writing a great novel.

"America would not be America without the big and small cities. I recently took a trip to a foreign country."

Ed paused. His eyes roamed through the great arena waiting for the words to come that would unlock what waited in his heart.

"When you go away from home, you miss the familiar patterns that make up the life you know. Breakfast with your wife. Taking a walk with your kids after dinner and showing them the stars. The hometown paper, your barber, and the greetings of the people when you arrive at work. These are little things. But in America these little moments have a richness and vitality missing elsewhere.

"Do you know why? Because America is still the land where everything is possible. In America, when a parent talks with a child, they may speak of the present, but the future hovers over them like a promise.

"Coming home to the America I love I am reminded of America's greatness and America's uniqueness. It is the vitality of America that makes her great. Some of that vitality comes from our people. But much of that vitality comes from the laws and institutions of America that set us free to come alive and make the future keep its promises. We must safeguard the flame that is at America's core, the flame of creativity, of change, of life. God bless you, and God bless Frank Bates. Good night!"

The crowd roared its approval, but I wasn't sure what or whom they were applauding. Probably a little of Ed Johnson, a little of Frank Bates, and a lot of America. When the crowd finally settled down, people tried to understand how Ed's speech fit in with Frank's protectionism. Some found a link between protectionism and protecting the American way of life. But others said Ed had never mentioned protectionism and maybe had denied its virtues. They couldn't understand why he'd thrown away the end of his speech to speak about America's greatness. They said he betrayed Frank Bates.

I thought he had. I might have wished for a more direct statement about the evils of tariffs and quotas, but sometimes the roundabout way is best....

CHAPTER FOURTEEN

A Final Word from David Ricardo

Did Ed Johnson betray Frank Bates? A tough call. A young fellow out of Massachusetts got the nomination that year and went on to the White House. Frank Bates ran for Congress again the next time around and lost narrowly. Did Ed Johnson destroy Frank's career? I think not, though Ed's speech didn't help Frank. It was a tightrope act from a man trying to keep the respect of a politician and his respect for himself. Most people couldn't understand the speech and chalked it up to political naiveté. Blamed Frank Bates for letting a businessman address the convention and toss away the end of a speech Frank Bates's boys had written.

Some people blamed Ed anyway. Frank did. Never spoke to him again, which was probably fine with Ed. Ed retired from the television business. Sold his company to the Japanese on the promise that they keep the plant in operation for at least three years to give his workers a chance to look elsewhere.

Some people called Ed names behind his back and to his face. Ed took the worst of it with a smile. He lost some friends. Some never understood, didn't want to understand, and even Ed might have had difficulty explaining himself. Finally he stopped trying and contented himself with his wife, his hobbies, and taking trips to Boston and California to see his grandchildren.

As for me, perhaps my story holds as much interest for you as Ed Johnson's. I wish I could tell you the details, but I've signed a variety of pledges promising to keep the details private. You know how they are Upstairs. Free will and all that. I can tell you that things have turned out a bright bit better than I thought possible. What's it like? I'm afraid I can't say. I can tell you that Ed's speech has gotten me over some hurdles, but there are more still to come. The afterlife is like life that way. Just when you think you've reached the top, another set of peaks rises on the horizon. They ask more of some; less of others. So it goes.

I am allowed to tell you one spot of information. The key for my defense was that point about choosing life. Not the way you might think, getting in good with the Boss by quoting one of his favorite books. It doesn't work that way Upstairs, you know. No, the key was getting away from the economics, narrowly defined by standard of living. Don't misunderstand—I had the economics on my side. But money isn't everything. I'll tell you a secret that my pledges don't cover: economists understand better than anyone that it's not really about money, but about striving and living and dreaming.

If my story has given you any pleasure, I would ask one favor of you. Since my time as an economist, it has become fashionable to mock my profession for our alleged indecisiveness and the splits in our ranks over various questions. I may have done a poor job explaining the ideas of comparative advantage to the students of the world. But I have had much success with the economists. Even those who make theoretical arguments against free trade are loath to advocate tariffs and quotas in practice. So at the next cocktail party when someone tells a joke about the one-armed economist being unemployed because he can't say 'on the other hand' or how if you laid all the economists end to end, they still wouldn't reach a conclusion, don't encourage them with the false laughter such dull-wittedness provokes. Smile a knowing smile and tell them that you have heard otherwise on the question of international trade and from a very old, but reliable source.

To all those who lie awake across America thinking of what might be—sweet dreams.

CHAPTER FIFTEEN

Explanations and Further Reading

Star, Illinois

There is no town of Star in Illinois. The Stellar Television Company never existed. However, between 1948 and 1974, Motorola ran a television factory in Quincy, Illinois, producing Quasar televisions. They sold that plant to Matsushita in 1974 on the promise that they would keep the plant in Quincy. Matsushita closed the plant in 1976, citing poor conditions in the television industry. They kept in operation another plant purchased from Motorola in Franklin Park, Illinois, and continue to do so.

The town of Quincy had about 42,000 people in 1960. At its peak, the Motorola factory employed about 3,000 workers and made about 2,000 television sets a day. In 1990, Quincy's population was 39,000.

I have used employee reminiscences and stories of the Motorola plant in Quincy as background and inspiration for Star and the Stellar Television Company. I am grateful to Doug Wilson and Judy Nelson, News Editor and Librarian respectively, of the *Quincy Herald-Whig* for background information and sources. I am grateful to Lois Tyer, reference librarian at the Quincy Public Library, for reading me a story about the reunion of Motorola workers, five years after the plant closed. I thank Robert Meyer, former Assistant Superintendent of Quincy High School, for his memories of the effect that the plant closing had on the kids of Quincy.

I am grateful to the workers from the plant who spent time talking to me: Joy Viar, former line supervisor; Robert Morris, former foreman; Carl Swed, former plant manager; Lee Webster, former engineer; Steve Moody, who worked on the receiving dock; Donna Moody, former cafeteria worker; Jane Slater, whose jobs in the plant included wiring and soldering and key operator; Joanne Felker, former bookkeeper; Oneta Burner, former cook and cashier in the cafeteria; and Chris Schork, who did a variety of tasks in accounting, inventory, and payroll.

These former workers still have a strong loyalty to Motorola and gratitude for the years they spent working in the plant. One of them told me that her husband would not take the road by the plant when she was in the car, because she would start to cry. They all felt Motorola was a fair and good employer. They spoke with fondness of the dances, skating parties, and the company picnic. None spoke bitterly about the sale of the plant to the Japanese, though some resented the Japanese for closing the plant. While all expressed varying degrees of sadness on the plant closing, the common assessment was that most workers found work within a year of the closing.

The Broadcast Electronics Company opened a plant in Quincy after about a year and employed some of the laid-off workers. I wish to thank Cathy Ellerbrock and Steve Wall of Broadcast Electronics for putting me in touch with former Motorola workers. Others found work in town at the Harris Allied Broadcast Company and MicroENERGY. Some of the workers found new work at a Ford seat belt factory across the river in Missouri, that closed after a few years.

Lee Webster, who had been an engineer at Motorola, eventually became plant manager at MicroENERGY. He told me that MicroENERGY produces custom power supplies for computers such as Motorola, Zenith, and Texas Instruments. While they do not sell directly to Japan, some of their products get to Japan as power supplies for NCR computers sold there.

Everyone I spoke to felt that the loss of the Motorola plant was a tough blow for Quincy, but everyone felt that their children, the next generation of Quincy, were better off than they were. As one put it, "They may sing the blues, but they have everything. Two cars. A house full of furniture. Some even have a boat." One former worker said that most of the college-educated kids don't find opportunities in Quincy, and instead settle elsewhere. The most revealing comment I heard that relates to the arguments of this book was an assessment of the virtues of working at Motorola. "It was a stable family atmosphere. There was no point in getting extra education for a different job you might not like."

Clearview, Illinois

There is no town of Clearview, Illinois. I have drawn inspiration for Clearview from the town of Arcola, Illinois. The September 7, 1992, *St. Louis Post Dispatch* ran a story on the North American Free Trade Agreement and the broom industry, highlighting the threat to the Libman Broom Co. of Arcola. I spoke with one of the owners, William Libman, who told me of his trips to Washington to fight NAFTA. Employees at the plant whom I spoke with on the phone estimated that half of the workers were either Mexican or the children of Mexicans who came to the plant beginning in the 1960s when companies from Arcola went to Mexico in search of broomwinders.

The September 24, 1993, *New York Times* ran a story on NAFTA and the France Broom Co. in Paxton, Illinois. I spoke with an employee there who told me that the company employed no Mexicans. But he told me that they did contract out some work to intermediaries, one of which was located in Arcola, who hired a lot of Mexicans. When I asked him why Arcola had so many Mexicans, he confirmed the story that companies had "imported" Mexicans many years earlier and that word of mouth among friends and relatives about wages in Arcola helped increase the size of the Mexican population.

Liberties

To dramatize the choice facing Ed Johnson and America I have taken various liberties. America has changed a lot since 1960 and all of those changes are not due to the relatively open borders of the United States with the rest of the world. I doubt that restricted trade policies would have left small town America unchanged. Nor is the increased labor force participation of women, for example, due to the relatively open borders of the United States between 1960 and today. The explosion of women's labor force participation does illustrate the flexibility of labor markets to respond to change. I apologize to the Democratic Party for what may be historical inaccuracy. In 1960, Frank Bates may have more likely been a Republican. Today, protectionism finds a readier home in the Democratic Party, so I have made Frank Bates a Democrat to jar the modern reader.

It is important to remember that the real America of 1993 is not a world of free trade. America has thousands of tariffs and quotas on a stupendously detailed array of products. While the average tariff in the United States is around 5%, numerous products for quirky or political reasons have tariffs that are quite high, including 32% for brooms, 40% for orange juice, and 34.6% for polyester sweaters. In addition, as I discussed in Chapter Eleven, antidumping laws allow tariff-like fees to be assessed without politicians having to vote for them. Such fees are depressingly numerous.

Facts and Figures

I placed Ed Johnson in 1960 because that was the beginning of the surge in Japanese television imports. I have tried to take data from 1992 where possible or to make comparisons between 1960 and 1990. Otherwise, I have used the most recent data available or used the dates authors have used for their studies.

In Chapter Four I discuss the improvement in the American standard of living between 1960 and 1990. Many people believe that the United States is in decline or stagnation. Some have even argued that this goes back to 1960 and blame this on the Japanese. I believe this is an impossible case to make on either theoretical or empirical grounds. Hourly wages are an admittedly crude measure. Demographic effects, immigration, and government taxes and regulation all affect wages and compensation in complex ways.

The figures on hourly wages of 2.09 in 1960 and 10.02 in 1990 are from Table B-42 of the 1992 Economic Report of the President, taken from the Bureau of Labor Statistics. The real change is 19%. I deflated with the CPI-U-X1 found in the Department of Commerce's "Money Income of Households, Families, and Persons in the United States," from 1991. The CPI-U-X1 corrects the standard CPI by trying to measure the rental cost of housing.

To get a measure of worker compensation inclusive of fringe benefits, I have used Table B-44 from the 1992 President's Report, also from the Bureau of Labor Statistics. I have used hourly nominal compensation for the business sector, deflated by the CPI-U-X1. This shows an increase between 1960 and 1990 of 63%. Richard McKensie finds a similar increase in calculation for all workers in his *What Went Right in the 1980s*. See McKensie's book or the volume edited by Marvin Kosters, *Workers and Their Wages*, for more sophisticated analyses of the recent history of wages. Despite claims of a U-turn in wages, these authors find that American wages have grown in the 1960s, 1970s, and 1980s, though growth is slower in the later decades.

The figures on manufacturing wages and the proportion of payroll employees in manufacturing are taken from Tables B-42 and B-41 in the 1992 Report.

Readily available statistics such as the labor force participation of women, the number of jobs in the United States, and the proportion of workers in agriculture have been taken from a variety of sources including *Historical Statistics of the United States*, the *Statistical Abstract of the United States*, and the 1992 Economic Report of the President.

Many readers have been surprised by the statistics comparing United States and Japanese standards of living and trade patterns. Per capita income figures fluctuate wildly with currency fluctuations. In many of these calculations, Japan ranks ahead of the United States. A more accurate measure uses purchasing power parity. According to the World Bank's *World Development Report*, which uses purchasing power parity, the U.S. standard of living in 1990 is 25% above Japan's. Other estimates show similar results.

Per capita imports from the rest of the world for the United States and Japan are taken from the International Monetary Fund's data on imports in *International Financial Statistics*. In 1992, the United States imported $553.9 billion while Japan imported $233.2 billion. Using population estimates of 255 million for the United States and 125 million for Japan yields the per capita figures in the text. These figures exclude services. If they did not, I think the per capita numbers would be close to identical, but 1992 Japanese service imports are not readily available. The fact that the average Japanese imports about the same amount as does the average American is interesting in that it refutes common wisdom that Japan is virtually a closed market. There is nothing inherently good or bad about that near equality.

Data on trade between the United States and Japan are taken from the *Survey of Current Business*, June 1993. In 1992, the United States imported $110.9 billion worth of goods and services from Japan while Japan imported $72.9 billion from the United States. I thank Ed Leslie of the Department of Commerce for help with this data. Using population estimates of 255 million for the United States and 125 million for Japan gives the corresponding per capita figures of $435 and $583 that are alluded to in the text.

It may surprise the reader to know that I have only touched on the bizarre complexity of the Polish golf cart dumping case. More details can be found in 57 Federal Register 10334 (3/25/92). Figures on dumping cases between 1986 and 1992 are from telephone conversations with Keith Anderson of the United States International Trade Commission. The Chinese manhole story is from James Bovard's *The Fair Trade Fraud* which has a wonderful discussion of the medieval nature of the antidumping law. I also took information and statistics on dumping from Tracy Murray's and N. David Palmeter's articles in *Down in the Dumps: Administration of the Unfair Trade Laws*, edited by Richard Boltuck and Robert E. Litan. Further data on dumping cases and their distribution by country can be found in Keith Anderson's article "Antidumping Laws in the United States—Use and Welfare Consequences" in the *Journal of World Trade*, April 1993.

For two opposing discussions of the relative openness of Japan's markets to foreign products, see Robert Z. Lawrence's "Japan's Different Trade Regime: An Analysis with Particular Reference to Keiretsu," and Gary R. Saxonhouse's "What Does Japanese Trade Structure Tell Us About Japanese Trade Policy?" Both can be found in the Summer 1993 issue of *The Journal of Economic Perspectives*.

Background on the Concorde and HDTV was taken from various articles in the popular press. Data on the Concorde's fares were found by calling British Air on July 29, 1993. Round-trip on the Concorde, New York to London without advance reservations, was $7,019. British Air's regular fare without advance reservations for non-Concorde travel was $958.

I would have liked to have provided a more thorough discussion of high-definition television, but too much was going on as this book went to press. Unfortunately, the current Secretary of Labor, Robert Reich, and Congressman Richard Gephardt have argued for favoring the technology that produces the most jobs in the United States rather than the best technology. Ironically, this criterion will favor the analog-based European firms because they build televisions in Indiana and Pennsylvania. American firms backing the superior digital transmission will be handicapped. This is a beautiful—albeit depressing—example of how politics overrides even the best cases for industrial policy. So much for the importance of technology spillover. The contenders are negotiating, so there is hope that the best technology will come to market anyway.

The length of time a worker must toil to buy a television was calculated as follows. It is not easy to get actual retail prices in 1960. I used the 1960 Sears catalog. The cheapest 21" television that was able to receive both UHF and VHF sold for $180. The price of the cheapest remote control model was $380. Average weekly earnings in the manufacturing sector in 1960 were just under $90. So the average manufacturing worker needed two weeks of work to be able to buy a television. In 1990, a 20" color television sold in the Sears catalog for $290. Average weekly manufacturing earnings in 1990 were about $442. So in 1990, the average manufacturing worker had to work a little over 3 days to earn a television.

This comparison is biased against 1990 in many ways. The 1990 television is a color television of superior quality measured by reception and particularly by maintenance and durability. The worker in 1990 has a benefits package which is many times more generous than the worker in 1960. In addition, the worker in 1990 has more retailing choices. If he chose to buy his television through Circuit City, even in 1993, he could pay as little as $200 for a comparably sized television, lowering the days worked to about 2 1/4 days. So depending on how you define quality and price, you can actually make the case that the *nominal* price of televisions is lower in 1993 than in 1960.

The advantage of using weekly earnings in manufacturing is that hours worked per week are roughly the same in manufacturing in 1960 and 1990. If you use all private (non-governmental) workers, there is the confounding effect of the dramatically shorter work week for non-manufacturing jobs. Many things have changed between 1960 and today that affect the price of televisions. The point is to show how relying on foreign televisions does not appear to have increased their price.

Data on Hong Kong's experience in the 1980s was sent to me by John G. Greenwood, Chairman of G.T. Management (Asia) Limited. See his article, "Hong Kong, The Changing Structure and Competitiveness of the Hong Kong Economy" in the *Asian Monetary Monitor*, November/December 1990, for more data on Hong Kong.

The 1960 Democratic Party Convention was held at the Los Angeles Memorial Sports Arena from July 11-July 15.

According to Ward's Automotive Yearbook of 1962, the Ford Fairlane and Chevrolet Impala were the two best-selling cars of 1960, so I have let them persist into 1995 in a world without imports. The top selling cars in America today are the Honda Accord and the Ford Taurus. The 1960 Ford Fairlane got 14 and 19 mpg in the city and on the highway. The figures for the 1993 Honda Accord are 22 and 28; the 1993 Ford Taurus gets 22 and 27. I want to thank Tracie Tillinger of *Automotive News* and Ron Grantz, the curator of the National Automotive History Collection at the Detroit Public Library, for help in locating these figures and providing other background on the American car industry. I talk about the Accord as a foreign car. It was in its earlier days. For many years, now, the bulk of its production has been in Marysville, Ohio. Honda recently announced that all Accords will be made there.

Jason Vines of the American Automotive Manufacturer's Association was able to uncover the total number of production workers making cars and trucks employed by GM, Ford, and Chrysler. I thank him for his time and his dedication to accuracy.

I want to thank Susan MacKnight of the Japanese Economic Institute for her insights into the Japanese car market. The figures on foreign car sales in Japan are taken from the Institute's Report 27A, *U.S. Vehicle Sales in Japan: Perception Problems*.

I am grateful to Valarie Kusuda-Smick of Boeing for background on Boeing and a rough estimate of Boeing's annual sales to Japan. Because the number of airplanes in any one sale is large, the average will not be a good predictor for any one year.

Further Reading

I have tried to make any remarks about David Ricardo as accurate as possible. His classic work is *Principles of Political Economy and Taxation*. It is not light reading. A general textbook introduction to international trade is *World Trade and Payments* by Richard Caves and Ronald Jones. Jagdish Bhagwati's *Protectionism* is a good introduction to the specifics of trade policy that requires little background in economics. A delightful compendium of the ugly politics of trade policy is in James Bovard's *The Fair Trade Fraud*. He has some amazing examples of absurdity in America's trade policy and a superb catalog of the biases in the Department of Commerce's assessment of dumping. Kenichi Ohmae's *The Borderless World* has some excellent insights into trade issues from the other side of the Pacific. I thank Tatsuo Achiwa for bringing Ohmae's work to my attention.

In recent years, a number of economists have been making a theoretical argument against free trade. I have given my slant on these arguments in Chapter Ten. A formal exposition of these arguments can be found in Paul Krugman's *Rethinking International Trade*. Expositors of these theoretical ideas are usually opposed to trade restrictions or government subsidies in practice. Not so Laura Tyson. See her *Who's Bashing Whom* for policy prescriptions in favor of government involvement.

Acknowledgments

The Talmud says, "I have learned much from my teachers, more from my colleagues, and most of all from my students (Taanis 7a)." My general interest in trade began with Milton Friedman's *Capitalism and Freedom* and continued during my undergraduate years at the University of North Carolina with a course from James Ingram. His book *International Economic Problems* uses a metaphor of an import/export business as a factory which helped inspire my approach here.

In graduate school at the University of Chicago I was fortunate to learn about trade issues in my microeconomics class from Don McCloskey. His diagram of the dead-weight loss from tariffs greatly influenced my teaching and thinking. I have taught this analysis of the losses from tariffs to thousands of students in thirteen years of teaching at the University of Rochester, Stanford University, UCLA, and Washington University in St. Louis. Many of the questions asked by those students have found their way to the mouth of Ed Johnson. I am grateful to my students for their passion, questions, and interest.

George Stigler gave me an enormous dose of skepticism about industry statements on their motives for supporting government legislation. I am sorry he did not live to see this book. I would have loved to chat with him about David Ricardo.

I wish to thank Dan Gressel of Teleos Asset Management, Inc. (who always knew more about international economics than I did, and still does) for sharing his insights into international trade and for teaching me long ago to focus on quantities not price when examining welfare effects. I have also benefited from conversations on general issues of international trade and the topics of this book with Kent Kimbrough, John Lott, Jr., and Richard McKensie.

Many American companies excel in the international marketplace. I have chosen a handful to mention here. I have been lucky to hear first-hand from Roy Vagelos of Merck, John Pepper of Procter & Gamble, and Jim Schwartz of Mast Industries about the creativity and excellence of their companies. I thank them for the time they spent at the Olin School at Washington University with students and me.

I had helpful conversations with Eric Schuster of Motorola, Simon Bonita, Takehiko Hayakawa, and Noel Howard of Merck, Martin Nuechtern of Procter & Gamble, and Hendrik Verfaille and Scott Koehne of Monsanto about their companies.

I want to thank Steve Goodman for insights into the neckwear industry, and Zev Fredman for continued scholarship on Frank Sinatra which came in handy.

I am grateful to Stephen Dietrich of Prentice Hall for his faith and efforts. I thank Sally Denlow of Prentice Hall for her energy and enthusiasm, especially in the early going.

Thomas Egan, Rob Fruend, and Catherine Knoebel provided timely and accurate research to support many of the numbers in the book.

Friends, family, and colleagues gave me support and many helpful suggestions for improving the manuscript. I wish to thank Andy Akin, Marci Armstrong, Denise Dill, Zev Fredman, Steve Goodman, Lisa and Randy Harris, Ron Jones, Jennifer Chilton-Kallery, Richard Klein, Catherine Knoebel, Suki Kotler, Barbara and David Kupfer, Tammy Kupfer, Michael Levin, Pat Masidonski, Gary Miller, Stephen Moss, Jennifer and Joe Roberts, Shirley and Ted Roberts, Gregg Rotenberg, Bevis Schock, Phyllis Shapiro, Michael Wolkoff and Larry Zarin for their help. I wish to thank Alan Deardorff of the University of Michigan, Don Schilling of the University of Missouri, Pat Welch of St. Louis University, and Judy Ware of Crossroads School, along with their students, who used earlier versions of the book and gave me many helpful comments.

I want to thank my wife Sharon for her innumerable comments on innumerable drafts, her unflagging support, and her patience with my hours at the computer. She graciously took the less interesting role of Ed when we read portions of the manuscript to each other. Despite her formal skills in mathematics, she has refused to learn the graphs behind free trade and insisted instead on a mastery of the intuition. She has been a perpetual sounding board for the ideas I have tried to capture here. Any success this book has would be meaningless without her.

The birth of this book roughly paralleled that of our first child. As I write these words, Yael is almost six months old, and her hands have learned to reach and grasp. I hope the world she inherits gives her the opportunities for expression and wonder that would make David Ricardo proud.

About the Author

Russ Roberts teaches economics and is director of the Management Center at the John M. Olin School of Business at Washington University in St. Louis. He lives in University City, Missouri, with his wife and daughter.